Section 403(b) Compliance Guide for Public Education Employers

Fourth Edition

Ellie Lowder

Published in partnership with the
Association of School Business Officials International

ROWMAN & LITTLEFIELD EDUCATION

A division of
ROWMAN & LITTLEFIELD
Lanham • Boulder • New York • Toronto • Plymouth, UK

Published in partnership with the
Association of School Business Officials International

Published by Rowman & Littlefield Education
A division of Rowman & Littlefield
4501 Forbes Boulevard, Suite 200, Lanham, Maryland 20706
www.rowman.com

10 Thornbury Road, Plymouth PL6 7PP, United Kingdom

British Library Cataloguing in Publication Information Available

Library of Congress Cataloging-in-Publication Data

Lowder, Eleanor A., author.
  Section 403(b) compliance guide for public education employers / Ellie
Lowder. — Fourth edition.
     pages cm
  ISBN 978-1-61048-502-9 (cloth : alk. paper) — ISBN 978-1-61048-503-6
(pbk. : alk. paper) — ISBN 978-1-61048-504-3 (electronic) 1. 403(b) plans.
2. Deferred compensation—Taxation—Law and legislation—United States.
3. Annuities—Taxation—Law and legislation—United States. 4. School
employees—Taxation—Law and legislation—United States. I. Title.
  KF6425.L69 2014
  343.7305'23—dc23   2013033355

∞™ The paper used in this publication meets the minimum requirements of
American National Standard for Information Sciences—Permanence of
Paper for Printed Library Materials, ANSI/NISO Z39.48-1992.

Printed in the United States of America.

Contents

Reader's Note; Disclaimer

This guide has been prepared to provide accurate and reliable information to school business officials and is based on legislation, regulation, and guidance in effect at the time of preparation. However, it is not intended to provide tax or legal advice. Readers should consult legal or tax professionals for such advice.

The material in this guide cannot be used to avoid income and penalty taxes properly assessed by a United States taxing authority.

1

Introduction: What Is in This Guide?

What does this updated issue of the compliance book contain that previous versions did not contain?

IRS Plan Document Approval Program Posted

After a lengthy delay, the Internal Revenue Service posted Revenue Procedure 2013-22 (in April 2013), which provides the procedures (along with the List of Required Modifications, or LRMs, to be used as a guide in preparation of plan documents that are approved by the IRS) for gaining approval for either a prototype or a volume submitter plan document. Product providers, third-party administrators, and other organizations that make plan documents available are now expected to draft and submit plan documents for IRS approval. It is probable that IRS-approved documents will be available sometime in 2015, since the approval process is likely to be a lengthy one. School business officials (SBOs) will be alerted by their providers once each filing organization has received notice of approval of the submitted plan document. At that point, it will be important to review the available documents and consider the adoption of an approved document so that employers are assured that their document fully complies with IRS requirements.

In the revenue procedure, the IRS has made it clear that they will not be offering determination letters for individually designed plan documents (at least for the foreseeable future). This will mean that employers who desire to have an IRS-approved plan document will need to adopt either a prototype document or a volume submitter document.

New Correction Procedures Now Available

Additionally, Revenue Procedure 2013-12 was posted in 2013, with the most important change being the ability for employers to correct failure to adopt a 403(b) plan document on time. This ability will be of great interest to SBOs who failed to adopt a plan document no later than December 31, 2009, as required in the final 403(b) regulations and subsequent guidance. Prior revenue procedures did not permit the correction of failure to adopt a plan document on time. SBOs who are in that situation should obtain a copy of RP 2013-12 in order to correctly follow the procedures to file a submission under the Voluntary Correction Program to make that correction. It will be important to do so, since failure to adopt a written plan is one of the violations that could cause the entire 403(b) plan to be disqualified.

Grandfathered and Nongrandfathered Orphan Accounts

In Revenue Procedure 2007-71, the IRS provided model plan language (covered in chapter 5) and, even more importantly, identified which 403(b) accounts are required to be included in the employer's plan. This is of great importance as employers manage new compliance responsibilities, since not all 403(b) accounts in existence prior to January 1, 2009, are grandfathered. There will still be a need to include certain "preregulation" accounts in the employer's plan. That information is covered in chapter 5 in the section "Which 403(b) Accounts Must Be Included in the Plan?" Included in that chapter is the orphan account chart developed by the Association of School Business Officials (ASBO) Retirement Plan Council.

WHERE CAN EMPLOYERS GET ADDITIONAL INFORMATION ABOUT THE FINAL 403(b) REGULATIONS AND SUBSEQUENT GUIDANCE?

This book continues to incorporate the final 403(b) regulations; provides both explanation of the significant changes and a review of specimen forms and other resources prepared by the ASBO Retirement Plan Council (readily available at www.asbointl.org). Every effort is made in this edition to deal with myths versus facts in terms of interpreting the final regulations, as well as suggested best practices for continuing to maintain a 403(b) plan without extensive administrative burden.

As further explained in subsequent chapters of this guide, ASBO has developed a 403(b) Resources Center (at www.asbointl.org) that includes a number of informational pieces, a sample written plan, and other sample forms for employers to utilize as a guide. Additionally, many of the product providers and third-party plan administrators have prepared fact sheets and other resource materials for the specific use of school business and community college officials. Information is also available directly from the IRS website at www.irs.gov/Retirement-Plans (although that information may not deal with the practical steps that need to be taken, nor provide cautions on the pitfalls that might be encountered).

Naturally, any and all forms and documents should be carefully reviewed with legal counsel before use by the employer.

WHAT ELSE IS INCLUDED IN THIS EDITION?

All Other Relevant Legislation and Regulation
Available through July 2013

This edition also includes the changes made in the Pension Protection Act of 2006, including the very important removal of the sunset provisions of the Economic Growth and Tax Relief Act of 2001, in which the retirement plan changes were scheduled to expire on December 31, 2010 (which would have reinstated a number of very complex and difficult-to-manage requirements, especially in determining contribution limits for employees), as well as a few other important changes in other legislation that became law since the third edition was published.

HOW IS THIS GUIDE ORGANIZED?

Virtually every chapter of the fourth edition of the guide has been revised—or rewritten altogether—to reflect all of the myriad details of the final regulations and subsequent guidance. Only chapter 10, "The

Basic Rules for 403(b) Plans," has changed little (except that the contribution limits for the tax year 2013 are incorporated). Each chapter reflects a key element of the current regulatory environment, while in the later chapters, checklists and information about forms and agreements are shared.

457(b) Deferred Compensation Information Included

Additionally, as more and more public school districts and community colleges are adopting 457(b) deferred compensation plans, there is expanded information on those plans, including the similarities and the differences between 403(b) plans and 457(b) plans. A compliance checklist for 457(b) plans will also help readers as they meet compliance requirements for those plans.

2

Overview: Final Regulations; Extension of Written Plan Adoption Date

THE FINAL 403(b) REGULATIONS

The most significant change in the history of 403(b) plans is the final 403(b) regulations, posted on July 27, 2007, with an effective date for most public education employers of January 1, 2009. For certain 403(b) plans that are collectively bargained, there may be a later effective date; however, the vast majority of public school districts and community colleges must meet new requirements on and after the earlier date. Subsequent chapters provide more detail on the elements of the final regulations that impact public education employers as well as all of the basics of 403(b) plans that already existed outside the boundaries of the regulations.

Note that the bulk of the final regulations does not actually impose change (other than the requirement that employers must have a written plan); it simply ties together the rules and regulations imposed by a number of IRS notices, revenue rulings, and revenue procedures that have formed the basis of 403(b) rules since the last set of comprehensive regulations was posted over forty years ago. However, the regulations have a substantial impact; they change the 403(b) "programs" of public education employers to 403(b) "plans," creating new responsibilities for employers.

EXTENSION OF DATE ON WHICH WRITTEN PLAN MUST BE ADOPTED

On December 12, 2009, the Internal Revenue Service posted Notice 2009-3 (also covered in chapter 5), which simply provided that the written plan could be adopted as late as December 31, 2009, provided that the employer, during 2009, operated under the terms of that written plan once adopted. The effective date of the written plan must be January 1, 2009. Thus, the extension simply permits employers that could not get the written plan in place prior to January 1, 2009, some additional time to formalize the terms of the plan. The guidance also liberalizes slightly the operation of the plan under the final regulations by providing that employers can use a "reasonable interpretation" of those regulations in the operation of the plan in 2009. If operational failures occur during 2009, employers can correct those failures retroactively to January 1, 2009, under the principles of IRS correction programs (covered in chapter 15).

**Understanding That Preexisting Accounts
Must Be Included in the Plan**

In late November 2007, the IRS provided guidance in Revenue Procedure 2007-71 on which "preregulation" 403(b) accounts are required to be included in the compliance responsibilities imposed by the final regulations. The definitions of grandfathered accounts for which the employers have no responsibilities versus the nongrandfathered accounts that require a reasonable good-faith effort for the sharing of the information necessary to meet the compliance standards are covered in depth in chapter 5.

A CHANGE IN CULTURE

Since the inception date of 403(b) arrangements for public education employers (in 1961), 403(b) plans were regarded as simple arrangements in which employees could voluntarily set aside savings for retirement. Many of the 403(b) accounts held by employees are held in individually owned annuity contracts or custodial accounts invested in mutual funds.

With the changes in the final regulations, however, the Internal Revenue Service has imposed a written plan requirement in which the employer is given the responsibility of compliance with the rules and regulations of 403(b) in a plan environment. This is a substantial change from a program in which the employer was permitted to offer an excellent benefit to employees without substantial administrative burden.

HIGHLIGHTING THE CHANGES MOST AFFECTING PUBLIC SCHOOL DISTRICTS AND COMMUNITY COLLEGES

Plan Disqualification Events

The final regulations make clear that there are only three violations that are plan disqualification events (in which, if the plan is disqualified, all nongrandfathered accounts held in the plan would be disqualified accounts):

1. The employer is ineligible to sponsor a 403(b) plan. This, of course, would not be applicable to public school districts or community colleges, which are, in fact, eligible.
2. There is a violation of the universal availability rule (covered in detail in chapter 12).
3. The employer fails to adopt a written plan and operate the 403(b) plan under the terms of that plan.

If there are operational violations, such as a violation of contribution limits, loan limits, or hardship withdrawal rules, only the account or accounts of affected employees are potentially at least partially disqualified.

Compliance Responsibilities

The overall purpose of the final regulations is to shift the responsibility for compliance with the code and the regulations to the employer. While employers can delegate the management of those responsibilities to other parties, they cannot avoid the ultimate responsibility for proper management of their 403(b) plans.

Public school districts and community colleges have never had full responsibility before, and there has been much concern about how best to meet the requirements. There has also been misinformation about the purpose or the meaning of the regulations. As an example:

1. The final regulations do not require that employers select a limited number of product and investment providers—that decision is entirely up to the employer (with input from employees and their unions, where appropriate).
2. The final regulations do not cause public education employers to be subject to ERISA requirements. Retirement plans sponsored by public school districts, community colleges, and public colleges and universities are and continue to be altogether exempt from ERISA (ERISA 3(32)).
3. The final regulations do not impose fiduciary responsibilities on employers. The IRS has no authority (only ERISA or state statute can impose those responsibilities) and does not force employers to assume the role of a fiduciary. Chapter 7 discusses this issue in detail.

Written Plan

A written plan must be adopted no later than December 31, 2009, and, in operation, it must conform to the terms of that written plan. The single exception for public education employers will be an employer sponsoring a 403(b) plan that was collectively bargained in which the effective date is the earlier of the date on which the last of the elective bargaining agreements terminates, or July 26, 2010. The plan must include the following:

1. The conditions for eligibility, benefits, contribution limits (as permitted in the code), the providers included in the plan (on a separate addendum or administrative list), and the timing and form under which benefit distributions will be made.
2. The optional features included in the plan (such as loans, hardship withdrawals, plan-to-plan transfers, exchanges within the plan, and whether rollovers are accepted into the plan).
3. Identification of the party or parties selected to provide transactional support to meet compliance requirements (most often the providers of product, or a third-party plan administrator to which the employer has assigned transactional responsibility).

Much of the language in the written plan can refer to the underlying contractual language of the annuity contracts and custodial accounts offered by the approved providers in the plan. However, as noted in the IRS plan approval document, the plan terms will override the underlying contractual language.

Timely Remittance of Salary Reduction Contributions

Contrary to the rules in place prior to the effective date of the regulations, in which salary reduction contributions were required to be remitted no less than once each year, those contributions must now be remitted as soon as administratively practicable. In no event can the contributions be remitted later than the fifteenth business day of the month following the month in which the amount was taken from each employee's paycheck. Note that in many states, state statute requires more rapid remittance of those salary reduction contributions, in which case state statute must be followed.

Universal Availability

It is now required that employers must provide a meaningful notice of the right to participate and a meaningful opportunity to do so no less than once each year. "Meaningful" is interpreted to mean:

1. The notice must contain specific information about the plan, including how to enroll, make changes in providers, and change contribution levels.
2. The opportunity to participate or make changes must include ample time for employees to take advantage of the open period(s).

While certain employees can be excluded—for example, part-time employees not expected to or not having worked one thousand hours in the tax year (or the previous tax year)—employers should exercise caution in choosing such exclusions because if only one employee working less than those hours is permitted to participate, then all of the employees in that category must be permitted to participate. It is important to note that every common-law employee is eligible to participate, whether part time or full time. This topic is covered in detail in chapter 12.

Limitation on Tax-Free Transfers and Exchanges

Effective on September 25, 2007, it is no longer permissible for employees to transfer or exchange one 403(b) account for another 403(b) account if the recipient insurance or mutual fund company is not a part of an employer's plan. There are two ways to satisfy the inclusion of the recipient provider in the employer's plan:

1. By including that provider in the employer's written plan for the purposes of ongoing contributions.
2. By entering into an agreement to share the information necessary to meet compliance requirements with a provider that is not otherwise a part of the employer's plan (because the provider is approved to receive exchanges only).

Chapter 9 covers this topic in detail.

3

What Are the Employer's Options to Comply?

TWO OPTIONS

Employers can choose one of two viable options to comply with the final regulations. Both options reflect the final regulations, which clearly permit an employer to delegate the administrative responsibilities to someone other than the employer. (Even though the delegation of the details of compliance does not reduce the ultimate responsibility of the district or community college, assigning the handling of transactions to someone else permits the employer to become compliant without the need to maintain staff with specific expertise in the various sections of the Internal Revenue Code and all relevant regulations.) Additionally, it is a fact that the use of service provider agreements with proper indemnification language can result in reimbursement of amounts that the IRS might assess to the employer if the violation is the result of the service provider's failure to honor the terms of the agreement. A sample service provider agreement appears in chapter 19.

Option 1

Require that the providers that are included in the written plan agree to share information regarding transactions (such as loans and hardship withdrawals) with the employer and with the other providers in the plan to avoid violations. In this option, the employer would serve as the source of data (such as whether a specific employee has another account in the 403(b) plan, or an account in another plan that permits loans), then requiring that the provider verify with the other providers in the plan eligibility for that loan. Employers could require that the providers determine eligibility before permitting pre-59½ distributions or determine whether the employee has, in fact, severed employment or is eligible for a hardship withdrawal. Employers further would require that requests for loans or distributions be rejected by the providers when eligibility is in question.

Option 2

Contract with a 403(b) competent third-party plan administrator (TPA). The TPA would handle all transactions and, through written contract with the employer, would agree to assume the responsibility for complying with the requirements.

In considering which option works best for each specific employer, it is important to note that a TPA will generally charge fees for services, and employers will want to consider who will pay those fees.

IF A TPA IS USED

Include Compliance Services for the 457(b) Plan

It is important for employers to consider requiring that the TPA also provide compliance support for the employer-sponsored 457(b) plan. Many TPAs can, in fact, assist with both plans and with the coordination of transactions (where required) among the two types of plans.

Establishing the Credentials of a TPA

Employers will want to determine whether the TPA under consideration has experience in the management of compliance activities specifically for public school districts and community colleges, which are non-ERISA 403(b) plans—altogether different from certain plans sponsored by 501(c)(3) employers in which ERISA coverage applies. There are a limited number of independent TPAs who can demonstrate experience in the K–14 non-ERISA 403(b) plan segment, and these can best be vetted by checking references of other public school districts or community colleges using their services. It is also important to compare fees, since the fees charged by independent TPAs reportedly vary widely.

Additionally, it is important to confirm that the TPA under consideration has experience in the management of 403(b) compliance activities, not just 401(k) or other types of pension plans in which the rules are different.

Some Cautions in Selection of TPAs Involved in Product Sales

Employers should be cautious in the selection of service providers that are offering full-service plan administration without fees if those service providers also offer 403(b) products for sale. Numerous reports of this type of activity have revealed that certain providers have used private participant information obtained in the course of providing compliance services to promote and sell 403(b) products and investment options.

The selection of a TPA for employers who believe they need this service should include criteria to determine that there is no conflict of interest—that is, the employer may wish to ensure that the TPA does not also sell 403(b) products or agrees not to use information gained in compliance activities to sell products. There are, indeed, TPAs who specialize in providing compliance services for 403(b) plans that do not have such conflicts. Exercising this caution will avoid problems with employees who feel that their privacy rights have been violated with the sharing of information to meet compliance requirements, when, in fact, the information is used for an entirely different purpose.

Using the Available Resources in TPA Selection

Additionally, it is important to establish the general experience and competency of the TPA before final selection. In chapter 19, the "TPA Checklist: Questions to Guide Selection of a Third-Party Administrator" will be helpful in structuring the interview process, or an RFP for employers that prefer to utilize that approach. Employers may well be involved in the selection process from time to time in the future (if a change of TPA is contemplated, or if employers that originally chose to attempt to meet compliance requirements without a TPA find that contracting with a TPA makes sense).

4

Avoiding Compliance Responsibilities

It would be difficult, if not impossible, for employers to avoid the adoption of the written plan and the operation of the written plan in accordance with its terms. Some employers who feel they could not undertake the responsibilities, or, having undertaken the responsibilities, would prefer not to continue to do so, have asked whether plans could simply be frozen or, in fact, terminated altogether. There are difficulties with either approach.

1. The Internal Revenue Service has ruled that not all "preexisting" 403(b) accounts are grandfathered—and employers and providers holding those accounts are required to share information prior to the taking of distributions or loans. Thus, failure to adopt and conform to the terms of a written plan could cause nongrandfathered accounts to be disqualified. The simple discontinuance of ongoing contributions does not relieve the employer of compliance responsibilities.

2. Plan termination has not been accomplished unless the requirements for termination, as outlined in 1.403(b)-10, have been met by the employer. The most difficult requirement to meet is the requirement that all assets must be distributed from the plan as soon as administratively possible following the termination (generally, within twelve months of the termination). Since the majority of the assets held in the plans of public school districts and community colleges are reportedly held in individually owned annuity contracts or individually owned custodial accounts, the employer

has no authority (under most current contractual language) to order distribution. Since an individual employee may or may not agree to the distribution (perhaps because of surrender charges), it is highly unlikely that a plan can successfully be terminated. This could cause the accounts of the employees that received distributions to be treated as:

a. ineligible distributions, subject to taxes and potential penalty taxes; or

b. ineligible rollover distributions if rolled over.

POSSIBLE SOLUTIONS: PLAN TERMINATION

It is possible that the employer intent upon termination of the 403(b) plan could first survey all participants in the plan (this must include all nongrandfathered accounts of both current and former employees and/or their beneficiaries, as explained in chapter 5, to determine if each would individually agree to receive distribution). It would be important in any such communication to employees to explain that (1) distributions, if taken by all participants, are eligible for rollovers to IRAs or to another workplace plan, if any; and (2) distributions must be all or nothing. If every current and former employee (or beneficiary) does not agree, then the plan has not been properly terminated.

5

Structuring and Adopting the Written Plan; Understanding the Inclusion of Nongrandfathered Orphan Accounts

While the regulations do not specifically refer to the adoption of a plan document, it is clear that one single plan document is preferred by most employers. The alternative is to utilize other written instruments (such as salary reduction agreements, board resolutions, and the language in the underlying annuity contracts and custodial accounts that hold the assets of your plan), and then adopt a written plan-level instrument that ties all of those separate pieces together. Additionally, the final regulations do recommend, in the preamble, that the employer adopt one single written plan to accommodate multiple providers (not multiple written plans).

Finally, Revenue Procedure 2007-71 supplied certain model language for use by public school districts, certain portions of which are problematical, and with language only for elective deferral pretax contributions. For example, the model language supplied for public schools provides for automatic enrollment, while, in most states, statutes prohibit the taking of money from an employee's paycheck without the express authorization of that employee. Most employers, therefore, choose not to utilize the model plan language in its entirety.

WHAT THE WRITTEN PLAN MUST CONTAIN

The regulations require that the written plan include the following:

1. The optional features that you will include in your plan. This will include features such as loans, hardship withdrawals, in-service distributions at age 59½, the inclusion of the Roth 403(b) option,

employer (nonelective) contributions, transfers, exchanges, and the acceptance of rollovers into the plan. Remember that those features must be communicated to each of the product providers and to your employees.

2. All of the material terms and conditions for eligibility of employees to participate in the plan.

3. A list of the providers that you are including in your plan (as a separate addendum or administrative list so that you do not need to revise your plan document each time a provider is added or deleted).

4. The time and form under which distributions will be made (in many cases, the plan document will refer to the benefit options available in the annuity contracts or custodial accounts used in the plan).

5. Identification of the party (or parties) to which you have allocated the responsibility for performing the administrative functions necessary for compliance (this generally will be the providers of product, or a third-party plan administrator).

The sample plan document (available at www.asbointl.org) does include much of the model language.

It is important that the plan document be kept updated for future regulatory or legislative changes; thus, once adopted, employers should be alert to any changes that might need to be made—and, in fact, may wish to consider the adoption of a written plan provided by a third party that provides update services. Once the IRS-approved plan documents become available, the providers of those documents are required to provide amendments to plan documents when guidance or legislation makes those amendments a requirement.

THE TIMING AND PROCEDURE FOR ADOPTION OF THE WRITTEN PLAN

It is recommended by the Internal Revenue Service (in public forums) that each employer utilize an adoption agreement with signature by the party authorized to adopt the written plan. Generally, for most employers, this will be the governing board; however, it could be the party appointed by the board to take any and all actions necessary to offer and properly administer the 403(b) plan (such as the school business official). While the December 2008 guidance (Notice 2009-3) permits additional time for adoption of the written plan, it is highly recommended that employers who did not adopt the written plan prior to January 1, 2009, move quickly to do so. Why?

- The extension of time to put the written plan in place did not change the general effective date of the regulations. Thus, the employer must operate under a reasonable interpretation of the final regulations throughout 2009, and must, when the written plan is adopted, make it retroactively effective on January 1, 2009.
- If, during 2009, the employer does not conform to the requirements of the final regulations and the written plan, operational failures can be corrected utilizing the correction principles (see chapter 15) of the Employee Plans Compliance Resolution System.

It would be far easier to conform to the terms of the written plan if it is adopted before January 1, 2009—and, if not, adopted as early as possible in the 2009 calendar year. This will help avoid operational failures and the need to correct those failures under IRS correction procedures.

WHICH 403(b) ACCOUNTS MUST BE INCLUDED IN THE PLAN?

Certain 403(b) accounts in existence prior to the January 1, 2009, effective date of the final regulations are grandfathered—others are not. The following detailed explanation will help employers understand the accounts for which compliance responsibilities will apply, and the accounts for which the employer bears no responsibility whatsoever. It is taken from the 403(b) Resources section of the ASBO website.

WHAT ARE YOUR SCHOOL'S RESPONSIBILITIES FOR ORPHAN 403(b) ACCOUNTS? GUIDANCE: REVENUE PROCEDURE 2007–71

Introduction

In Revenue Procedure 2007-71, which contains certain model language specifically for public education employers (see the ASBO Specimen Plan Document, which incorporates portions of that model language), the

IRS included previously unavailable guidance on 403(b) accounts held by a school's employees with investment providers that are not a part of the school's plan. ASBO members will be relieved to know that many of those accounts are grandfathered, which means that the school will have no direct responsibilities for those accounts under its 403(b) plan. The school may, however, find some of the investment providers maintaining these grandfathered accounts seeking, at a minimum, to confirm information regarding loans and hardship withdrawals under the plan.

However, certain accounts are not grandfathered, and the guidance does require certain actions on the part of the school sponsoring the plan. These issues are addressed below, both in brief bullet point format and in the tables that immediately follow. ASBO members will want to consider communicating with investment providers holding nongrandfathered accounts that are not a part of the school's 403(b) plan, as well as employees who may be holding nongrandfathered accounts so that those employees can consult with financial professionals prior to receiving loans or distributions from those accounts.

What Is an Orphan Account?

An orphan account is a 403(b) account held by the school's employee, former employee, or beneficiary that is not a part of the school's 403(b) plan on January 1, 2009 (or later, if the school's 403(b) plan is the result of a collective bargaining agreement). Certain orphan accounts are grandfathered, while others are not. For this purpose, an account with an investment provider that is deselected after January 1, 2009, is never a grandfathered orphan account: the contract remains in the school's 403(b) plan as long as the contract remains in force and continues to hold plan assets, unless the contract is transferred to another 403(b) plan or distributed out of the school's 403(b) plan (such as in a plan termination or at severance of employment).

Grandfathered Orphan Accounts

A school generally has no responsibility for including the following groups of grandfathered orphan accounts in the school's plan (the school's employees will deal directly with the investment providers of these accounts with no requirement that the school be directly involved—see table 5.1).

Table 5.1. Orphan Accounts for Which the School Has No Information Sharing Responsibility

Ongoing Contribution Accounts Held by Current Employees (Contributions Made before 2005 and Provider Deselected)	Accounts Held by Former Employees and Beneficiaries as of January 1, 2009 (Provider Deselected)	Accounts Transferred on or before September 24, 2007
• Contract held by current employee as of January 1, 2009 • Contract issued before January 1, 2005, and • No contributions to any contract held by the investment provider after December 31, 2004 (i.e., investment provider is not included under the school's plan) • No information sharing agreement is required • School has no responsibility for information sharing with the investment providers of these accounts. There need be no effort to include these investment providers in the school's 403(b) plan. • (The employee will deal directly with the investment provider holding the account, with no impact on the school's 403(b) plan. The investment provider may seek information from the school or other providers to comply individually with 403(b) regulations.) • If the school's 403(b) plan permits, employees can exchange these accounts to an investment provider that is a part of the school's plan or with which the school has entered into an information sharing agreement.	• Contract held by former employee or beneficiary as of January 1, 2009 • Contract issued before January 1, 2009 • Contract does not hold any assets of current employees as of January 1, 2009, and • Investment provider ceases receiving contributions to any contract on or before December 31, 2009 (i.e., investment provider is not included under the school's plan) • No information sharing agreement is required • School has no responsibility for information sharing with the investment providers of these accounts. There need be no effort to include these investment providers in the school's 403(b) plan. • (The former employee or beneficiary will deal directly with the investment provider holding the account, with no impact on the school's 403(b) plan. The investment provider may seek information from the school or other providers to comply individually with the 403(b) regulations, in particular prior to permitting loans from those accounts.)	• Contracts properly transferred under Revenue Ruling 90-24 on or before September 24, 2007 • No information sharing agreement is required • School has no responsibility for information sharing with the investment providers of these accounts. There need be no effort to include these investment providers in the school's 403(b) plan. • (The employee will deal directly with the investment provider holding the account, with no impact on the school's 403(b) plan. The investment provider may seek information from the school or other providers to comply individually with the 403(b) regulations.) • If the school's 403(b) plan permits, employees can exchange these accounts to an investment provider that is a part of the school's plan or with which the school has entered into an information sharing agreement.

- School employees' accounts held by investment providers (i.e., the insurance companies issuing the annuity contracts and the custodians holding the 403(b)(7) mutual fund investments) that were deselected before 2005 (i.e., the investment provider received no contributions made to any account of any of the school's employees after December 31, 2004).
- Accounts of individuals who were former employees or beneficiaries as of January 1, 2009, which are held by investment providers that were deselected prior to that date (although the providers may be seeking information prior to the granting of loans or hardship withdrawals).
- 403(b) accounts that were properly transferred to any investment provider (regardless of whether that provider was ever approved to receive contributions and whether that provider is part of the school's 403(b) plan after December 31, 2008) under rules in effect on or before September 24, 2007.

Nongrandfathered Orphan Accounts

The guidance indicates that a school must make a reasonable good-faith effort to include nongrandfathered accounts in compliance coordination protocols (also sometimes referred to as information sharing protocols) of your plan (see details provided in table 5.2). These nongrandfathered accounts include:

- All 403(b) accounts held by the school's current employees in which the investment provider has received contributions between January 1, 2005, and December 31, 2008, and that investment provider is not eligible to receive either contributions or exchanges under the school's plan as of January 1, 2009.

Correction of Improper Tax-Free Exchanges

- A 403(b) account improperly exchanged between September 25, 2007, and December 31, 2008, was permitted to be reexchanged before July 1, 2009, to an investment provider that is receiving ongoing contributions under the school's 403(b) plan, or with which

Table 5.2. Orphan Accounts for Which the School Has Information Sharing Responsibility

Ongoing Contribution Accounts Held by Current Employees (Contributions Made between January 1, 2005, and December 31, 2008, and Provider Deselected)—School Must Take Some Action

- Contract held by current employee as of January 1, 2009
- Contract issued on or after January 1, 2005, and before January 1, 2009, and
- Contributions made to account between January 1, 2005, and December 31, 2008, and
- Investment provider is not eligible to receive contributions or exchanges under school's 403(b) plan on or after January 1, 2009 (i.e., investment provider is not included under the school's plan)

As of January 1, 2009, the school must make a good-faith effort to contact such investment providers in an effort to exchange the information necessary to facilitate compliance. This may be accomplished by entering into an information sharing agreement or making other arrangements to share the information necessary for the proper administration of the school's 403(b) plan (including notifying the investment providers of the name and contact information for the person in charge of administering the plan).

The investment provider must make a good-faith effort to contact the school to exchange information before allowing a distribution or loan.

If the good-faith effort does not result in the exchange of necessary information, it is not entirely clear how these accounts are impacted. In its comment letter filed April 10, 2008, ASBO has requested that the IRS provide clarification on this issue. Updates will be provided to ASBO members on this and other issues when additional guidance is issued by the IRS.

If the school's 403(b) plan permits, employees can exchange these accounts to an investment provider that is a part of the school's plan or with which the school has entered into an information sharing agreement.

the school has entered into an information sharing agreement, and no information sharing is required for the intermediate contract. References to improper exchanges describe exchanges or transfers made to an investment provider which, on January 1, 2009, was neither an approved investment provider under the school's 403(b) plan nor an investment provider with which the school had entered into an information sharing agreement.

6

The Internal Revenue Service Plan Approval Program

A process to offer a program for approval of plan documents (a prototype or volume submitter plan document) was posted in early 2013, and the expectation is that preapproved documents should be available in 2014. It is anticipated that many product providers, third-party plan administrators, and document service vendors will file plan documents through that program, and then make those documents available to employers. Employers who choose to use a preapproved plan document will then enjoy plan amendment services that will alleviate any concern about whether the written plan continues to meet the requirements of the IRS. Using a preapproved plan document will also provide assurance to school business officials that their plan document will absolutely satisfy IRS requirements as to the form of the document. Adoption of the approved document also assures SBOs that the form of the document satisfies requirements retroactively to January 1, 2009. This retroactive satisfaction of plan document form is referred to by the IRS as the remedial amendment period.

Revenue Procedure 2013-22, which provides the guidance on submissions for document approval, also makes it clear that there will not be an IRS determination letter program that would provide an approval process for individually designed plan documents. Thus, SBOs who wish to utilize a plan document that has been approved by the IRS will need to use one of the preapproved documents provided by product providers, third-party plan administrators, or document service vendors.

While awaiting the approved documents (which, we are told, will be approved for the submitting vendors at the same time), it is perfectly permissible to use the plan document initially adopted to demonstrate the good-faith effort necessary to comply with the written plan requirement. However, if the initially adopted plan document has not been amended since it was adopted, SBOs will want to check with the provider of that plan document to determine whether amendments are needed.

7

ERISA and Fiduciary Issues

DO THE FINAL REGULATIONS CREATE ERISA OR FIDUCIARY RESPONSIBILITIES FOR YOU?

Reports continue that certain firms are telling public school districts that, with the final 403(b) regulations, they are now fiduciaries for their 403(b) plans. "Why," I am often asked, "am I being told I am a fiduciary? How can I protect my school district from misinformation?"

Despite the assertions of those firms, it is important to note that the final regulations make absolutely no change (and no reference whatsoever) to any assumption of fiduciary responsibilities. In fact, the Internal Revenue Service has no authority to impose fiduciary responsibilities on the sponsors of 403(b) plans.

Any fiduciary responsibilities that may apply to the sponsor of a 403(b) plan can only come from one of two sources:

1. ERISA: Employers subject to coverage under Title I of ERISA for their retirement plans are, in fact, fiduciaries. The retirement plans of public education employers, as governmental employers (as described in ERISA 3(32)), are exempt from Title I of ERISA altogether. Thus, the final regulations do not and cannot create ERISA coverage for any retirement plan (including the 403(b) plan) that you sponsor.
2. State statutes: While it is important to understand any statutes in your specific state that may impose fiduciary responsibilities for any retirement plans you sponsor, it is a fact that the final regulations cannot and did not change state statutes.

Employers that exercise caution not to assume a fiduciary role (unless the employer specifically wants to assume that role) and that were not fiduciaries prior to the final 403(b) regulations are still not fiduciaries.

COULD YOU TAKE ACTIONS THAT COULD CREATE NEW FIDUCIARY RESPONSIBILITIES?

If the employer simply selects or deselects the providers of products and investment options based on the simple criteria of whether those providers are willing and able to supply the necessary information to the employer (or the employer's designated responsible administrator of compliance activities), then there would likely be no assumption of a fiduciary role.

Alternatively, if the employer arbitrarily develops selection criteria based, for example, purely on low-cost offerings or arbitrarily moves from multiple provider selections to a single provider, many believe that the employer has assumed a fiduciary role. Other actions that could create fiduciary exposure would be to appoint an investment committee (or delegate that responsibility to a third party) to assume oversight of investment performance.

Employers should first carefully consider whether they wish to assume a role that might create fiduciary responsibilities or the assumption of potential exposures. If the answer is no, legal counsel should be consulted in order to gain a clear understanding of the statutes that may speak of the issue of fiduciary responsibility. Keep in mind that the assets held in your 403(b) plan are not required to be held in trust and thus are unlikely to be subject to state trust laws, which often impose fiduciary responsibilities (e.g., on plans such as the 457(b) plan that many public education employers also sponsor).

Caution: If employers are receiving advice from consultants to the contrary, it will be important to carefully check the credentials of the entity providing the advice. For example:

1. Can the consultant advising you that the final regulations impose fiduciary responsibilities supply the actual citation from those regulations that so state? Since there is no such citation in those regulations, can the consultant then provide the citations of the

statutes in your state that do impose such responsibilities, other than those that describe assets held in trust?

2. Does the consultant have experience specific to the non-ERISA 403(b) plans sponsored by public school districts and community colleges, or is the consultant's previous experience relevant only in the ERISA segment?

ASBO has available on its 403(b) Resources page (at www.asbointl. org, in the archives), a document that speaks in depth on the issue of fiduciary responsibility, prepared by the ASBO Retirement Plan Council. SBOs will find it helpful in working with legal counsel to clarify any fiduciary responsibilities in each specific state.

8

Selecting and Deselecting Investment and Product Providers and Third-Party Plan Administrators

NUMBER OF PROVIDERS REDUCED

Because of the impact of the final regulations, a number of insurance and mutual fund companies have signaled their inability to share the information necessary to meet the compliance requirements of the final 403(b) regulations. It is expected that others may, as time goes on, exit the 403(b) market. The reason requires explanation of the history of the K–14 market segment.

In the decades since 403(b) plans first became available to public education employers, there has, until now, never been a requirement that an annuity contract or custodial account be identified by employer. Thus, the companies offering 403(b) products generally did not establish systems that included record keeping on a plan level. There is a substantial cost to the development of such systems. Additionally, some companies have taken the position that they cannot share private participant data with anyone except the participant. For these reasons, the number of available product or investment providers has and may continue to decrease.

EMPLOYERS MUST MONITOR AND DESELECT PROVIDERS WHEN NECESSARY

There will be a need to impose strict requirements on the providers of annuities and custodial accounts, since it is absolutely essential that those providers exchange information with the employer or the employer plan administrator. This will be done through service provider agreements (see chapter 19), which employers must require that providers adhere to. The performance of providers under the terms of those agreements should be monitored, and employers should be prepared to eliminate (deselect) any provider that is not meeting those requirements. Not only must information necessary for compliance be provided, but that information must be provided in a format that is compatible with the employer's systems, processes, and procedures and, potentially, with a third-party plan administrator's systems, if one is used.

CAUTION: IRS NOTICE 2009-3

In light of IRS Notice 2009-3, which provided additional time to formalize the written plan (no later than December 31, 2009), it is important that employers understand that if any provider receives ongoing contributions on or after the general effective date of January 1, 2009, the employer must include that provider in the written plan when adopted. Failure to do so would cause the affected accounts to lose 403(b) status.

ADDITION OF NEW PROVIDERS

Over time, employers may want to add new providers to their 403(b) plan. Prior to those additions, the providers should be screened (using the service provider agreement as a tool in that screening process will quickly eliminate from consideration any provider that can't or won't cooperate); once screened, they should be added to the list of providers on the addendum to the plan document.

THE 403(b) FINAL REGULATIONS DO NOT
LIMIT NUMBER OF PROVIDERS

The final regulations simply require that employers and the providers of products or investments cooperate in the sharing of necessary information to meet the compliance standards. Additionally, the employer must list the approved providers as an addendum to the written plan and must limit ongoing contributions only to the providers that have agreed to cooperate with the compliance initiative. It is important to note that providers can be listed on more than one addendum. Employers may wish to list those receiving ongoing contributions (because those providers, under the terms of the written plan, have agreed to meet compliance standards necessary to receive those contributions) and a separate list of providers approved to receive exchanges only. The providers that are permitted only to receive exchanges (of one 403(b) account for another account within the employer's plan) must have an information sharing agreement executed with the employer. See chapter 9, where exchanges are explained.

Because 403(b) plans sponsored by K–14 employers have traditionally permitted multiple providers, the final regulations do recommend that, for multiple providers, a single plan document be utilized; however, they make no other reference to the selection of providers in the plan.

Additionally, it is important to note that deselection of product providers should be done only when the specific provider will not cooperate with the employer's compliance program, since the employer is taking that step to protect the tax status of the employees' accounts. Deselecting providers for noncompliance reasons may cause participation rates to substantially decline, as evidenced in a study done by Purdue University and the Association of Pension Professionals and Actuaries (ASPPA). Employers can view that study online at SaveMy403b (savemy403b.com).

REGULATIONS DO NOT REQUIRE THE EMPLOYER TO MONITOR INVESTMENT PERFORMANCE

The Internal Revenue Service has no authority to, nor do they, speak to the need for the employer to assume the role of monitoring the investment performance of the options available in the plan. Employers should carefully consider whether they wish to assume that role. Refer to the ERISA and Fiduciary Q&A link listed in chapter 19 to review carefully the concerns any employer might have in assuming a potential fiduciary role, if in fact the employer does not wish to do so.

9

Tax-Free Transfers, Exchanges, and Rollovers

DEFINITIONS

Transfers and Exchanges

Under the final regulations, new requirements and new terminology have been imposed, and the following definitions describe that new terminology:

- There are two types of transfers:
  1. The movement of one 403(b) account from a former employer's plan to a 403(b) account of a new or former employer's plan
  2. The transfer of 403(b) or 457(b) plan assets to the state retirement system defined benefit plan to purchase service credits
- "Exchange" is the movement of one 403(b) account to a 403(b) account offered by an approved provider in the employer's plan

Transfers and exchanges are not distributions; thus, no income tax reporting requirements apply.

Rollovers

While the final regulations do not change the rollover rules, it is important to understand that there is a need for employers to confirm eligibility of employees to receive a distribution prior to rollover of that distribution (as is further explained in this chapter).

- A rollover is the movement of eligible distributions from one plan type to another—or to or from an IRA. A rollover is a distribution and must be reported on Form 1099 and the taxpayer's tax return (even though not taxable if rolled over).
- Generally, distributions from accounts consisting of elective deferrals under the code are permitted at age 59½ or upon severance of employment. Different rules may apply to accounts consisting of employer (nonelective) contributions. Plan documents must specify the restrictions that will apply for contracts issued after January 1, 2009.

RULES AND REQUIREMENTS FOR TAX-FREE PLAN-TO-PLAN TRANSFERS

The transferring plan must permit transfers out of the plan, and the recipient plan must accept transfers in.

No information sharing agreements (ISAs) are required. The benefit following the transfer must be undiminished; however, it is permissible for product surrender charges to be applied by the transferring provider, and any applicable new product fees to be charged by the recipient provider. Additionally, the recipient provider must agree that any withdrawal restrictions applying to the account prior to the transfer must be at least as restrictive after the transfer.

RULES AND REQUIREMENTS FOR TRANSFERS TO PURCHASE SERVICE CREDITS

There is no required employer involvement in the movement of a portion (or all) of the assets from a 403(b) or 457(b) account to the state retirement system to buy years of service. As long as the employer's written plan permits transfers, employees are free to obtain the necessary information and paperwork from each respective state retirement system, then proceed with the transfer directly through their provider. The ability to purchase years of service with transfers from the 403(b) plan appears in Code Section 403(b)(13) and was not impacted by the final 403(b) regulations.

RULES AND REQUIREMENTS FOR TAX-FREE EXCHANGES

All exchanges made on and after September 25, 2007, are limited to recipient providers that are a part of the employer's plan. Unlike the pre–final regulations rules, it is no longer permissible for exchanges to be received by providers that are not (1) receiving ongoing contributions on and after January 1, 2009, or, (2) if not receiving ongoing contributions on and after that date, have in place an ISA with the employer.

Just as is true of transfers, the benefit following the exchange must be undiminished, and the withdrawal restrictions must be as great after the exchange as before.

Other requirements for tax-free exchanges:

1. The employer's written plan must permit exchanges.
2. The recipient providers must be confirmed as approved by the employer to receive exchanges.

USING THE INFORMATION SHARING AGREEMENT

The Internal Revenue Service does not require ISAs unless an exchange from one 403(b) provider to another 403(b) provider took place between September 25, 2007, and December 31, 2008, when the recipient provider is not, on and after January 1, 2009, a part of the employer's plan.

However, many employers utilized ISAs to quickly determine which providers would cooperate in the overall information sharing required to meet the compliance requirements imposed by the final regulations. If employers wish to continue to utilize that ISA to screen new providers before adding them to their plans, they can use the sample ISA prepared by the ASBO Retirement Plan Council. Note that chapter 19 contains a description and instructions on how to download that ISA sample.

CORRECTING IMPROPER EXCHANGES

For employees who exchanged a 403(b) account to a provider that, as of January 1, 2009, is not a part of the employer's plan (either because the recipient provider is not receiving ongoing contributions or has not, as of January 1, 2009, entered into an ISA with the employer), the guidance in Revenue Procedure 2007-71 permitted a reexchange if it was done no later than June 30, 2009. Thus, employees who would otherwise have had a tax consequence for the improperly exchanged account were permitted to correct the improper exchange (as long as the employer's plan permitted exchanges) with an exchange of that account for one with a provider that is a part of the plan.

ROLLOVERS

Rollovers Out of the Plan

Any employee eligible to receive a distribution at age 59½ (as long as the written plan permits in-service distributions) or upon severance of employment must be given the right, as well as notice of that right, by the product providers to directly roll over that distribution (either to an IRA or to another workplace plan, if any). The employer has no involvement other than to confirm that (1) the employee has left the employer, or (2) that the written plan permits in-service distributions at age 59½. Distributions are also permitted for employees that meet the disability requirements in the code, and those distributions are also potentially eligible for rollover treatment.

Rollovers into the Plan

Under the pension portability rules, amounts from other plan types or IRAs are eligible to be rolled into the 403(b) accounts held under the plan, provided that the written plan permits rollovers into the plan. Thus, employees who have retirement plan accounts with former employers (such as 401(k) accounts), or who have traditional IRA accounts, can consolidate those amounts with the 403(b) account held under the plan of the employer. The employer will need to confirm that the written plan permits rollovers into the plan, and the recipient providers will then be responsible for meeting the requirements for acceptance of those rollovers. The providers will further be responsible for segregating the amounts rolled into the plan (if the written plan requires segregation of those amounts). Note that segregation of those amounts conserves the employee's right to receive withdrawals from those rolled-over amounts without withdrawal restrictions. If the rolled-over amounts are not segregated, then the pre-59½ withdrawal restrictions applicable to 403(b) plans would apply. Employers should be sure to include that language in the written plan document to conserve the employee's right to make withdrawals from the amount rolled into the plan.

10

The Basic Rules for 403(b) Plans

Section 403(b) arrangements have been available to public education institutions since 1961, and it is estimated that the 403(b) accounts owned by some 9 million participants hold as much as $800 billion in assets. A Spectrem Group survey (reported in September 2008 by Plan Sponsor) reports that 52 percent of 403(b) plan participants describe themselves as very or somewhat conservative, compared to 41 percent of 401(k) plan participants, perhaps explaining why the largest percentage reportedly hold their assets in annuities, where underlying guarantees are available. Additionally, the participation rate in 403(b) plans is less (in the public school district and community college segment) than in 401(k) plans, most likely because the majority of 401(k) plans offer employer matching contributions—something that is generally not the case with the 403(b) plans sponsored by K–14 employers. This may also explain why the participation rates in 403(b) voluntary salary reduction plans are less than the 401(k) counterpart—with participation estimates in public schools and community colleges somewhere in the 40 percent range versus some 74 percent in 401(k) plans.

While no current studies are available, reports from various school districts around the country tell us that the estimated 40 percent participation rates in prior studies may have dropped, with many reporting that only 18–20 percent of eligible employees actually participate in their plans. The IRS has expressed concern about the low participation rates (covered in depth in chapter 12) and in current audits is reportedly asking employers how they are providing effective opportunity in terms of employee education programs to encourage greater numbers to participate in their plans. Chapter 12 offers more information, including the planning of an employee education program.

ERISA COVERAGE/NONDISCRIMINATION RULES

Retirement plans (including 403(b) plans) sponsored by public education employers are exempt from coverage under Title I of ERISA. This exemption applies in all cases, even when the employer is making nonelective employer contributions. Thus, the fiduciary and reporting requirements of ERISA do not apply to K–14 employers.

Employer contributions to a 403(b) plan sponsored by public education employers are also exempt from the nondiscrimination rules and testing that apply to other types of employers.

ELIGIBLE EMPLOYERS

Sponsorship of 403(b) plans is limited to two major types of employers:

1. Public education institutions, including K–12 public schools, community colleges, state colleges and universities, and the Department of Education. Most charter schools are also a part of the public education system, even though many carry the 501(c)(3) designation. Charter school officials should take care to determine if their specific charter school is a part of the public education system in each state.
2. Organizations with 501(c)(3) status, including such groups as hospitals, charitable and community services groups, religious organizations, and other employers who are organized to provide "religious, charitable, scientific, literary, educational or safety testing" services to the general public. As previously stated, this guide focuses only on the 403(b) plans sponsored by public education employers.

ELIGIBLE EMPLOYEES

Any employee of an eligible employer can participate in a 403(b) plan, with the exception of leased employees (because the IRS Code and related regulation does not specifically address leased employees in terms of 403(b) plans) and certain elected officials (more below). Independent contractors (outside service providers such as accountants, lawyers, or payroll processing firms) are not eligible to participate in the 403(b) plan.

Usually, elected officials cannot participate in the 403(b) plan. However, the exception will be an elected state or county superintendent because that individual is required to have a background in education in order to serve in the elected position. Individuals such as members of the board of regents of state university systems are not eligible to participate, because a background in education is not a condition of the elected position. Additionally, in instances when school board members receive compensation reported as wages on Form W-2, it is a fact that the elected official is still not eligible to participate in the 403(b) plan because this is an elected office for which no background in education is required. Additionally, the member of the governing board would not meet the definition of a common-law employee in which the employer can hire, fire, and set working hours and conditions of employment.

HOW CONTRIBUTIONS MUST BE MADE

Contributions made by employees can be made only through salary reduction of amounts that are not yet paid or made available. Employee contributions are reported by the employer on each employee's Form W-2.

Employee contributions are permitted during employment and from certain types of severance pay, as long as paid by the end of the tax year of severance or, if later, within two and a half months following severance of employment. The types of severance pay from which deferrals can be made after employment ceases are as follows:

1. Unused leave pay (because the unused leave would have been available for use had the employee not left)
2. Job performance pay, back pay, or bonuses (that would be paid whether the employee stayed or left)

Severance pay that is paid only if the employee leaves (such as early retirement incentive pay or contract buyout pay) is eligible for deferrals to the 403(b) plan only if paid while the employee is still employed.

Employers may elect, however, not to pay severance pay as cash but instead to make employer contributions to the 403(b) plan for the impacted employees.

Employer contributions (which are being made by many school districts and community colleges across the country) are simply made by the employer by directing the check for payment to each employee's 403(b) account. There is no Form W-2 reporting of employer contributions. Employer contributions are permitted during employment and for up to five tax years following the tax year in which employment is terminated (as further explained in chapter 13).

ELIGIBLE INVESTMENT OPTIONS

Contributions to the 403(b) plans of public education employers are limited to the following:

1. Section 403(b)(1) annuities: The annuities must be issued by life insurance companies and can be either fixed or variable contracts. Variable annuities, according to statistical data, appear to be the most popular of the available options offered in this market, perhaps because certain guarantees are available that are generally not available in mutual funds.
2. Section 403(b)(7) custodial accounts: Domestically traded retail mutual funds are permitted as a 403(b) option, provided that they are held in a custodial account.
3. Life insurance: While it is permissible to include life insurance (subject to specific limitations) in 403(b) annuity contracts, the final regulations prohibit the use of separate life insurance contracts in the 403(b) plan. A separate life insurance contract issued on or before September 23, 2007, is grandfathered and can continue to be funded; however, no new contracts can be included after that date.

The use of life insurance in an annuity contract is subject to limitations of no more than 25 percent of the contributions earmarked for universal or term life, and under 50 percent for whole life insurance. The actual cost of the life insurance death benefit can be purchased only with after-tax dollars. Reports are that many employers do not permit life insurance to be included in their 403(b) plans because of concerns about the more stringent requirements and the potential for violation of those requirements.

SPECIFIC LANGUAGE REQUIRED

The annuity contracts and the custodial account are required to contain specific language relative to nontransferability, the limits on elective deferrals, stipulations as to required minimum distributions, and limitations on withdrawals prior to attainment of age 59½ or severance of employment. Approved language relative to direct rollover options for eligible rollover distributions is also a requirement for the annuity contracts or the custodial account. Note that a direct rollover option must be provided for all eligible rollover distributions—that is a matter of law not impacted by final regulations.

Employers will want to require that the providers of annuity contracts for custodial accounts certify that the options they will offer to employees do contain the language that qualifies them to be options for a 403(b) plan. Additionally, with the written plan requirement, employers can refer to the underlying language in the annuity contracts or custodial accounts to describe many of the benefits and features available.

Finally, with the written plan requirement, it is expected that the insurance and mutual fund companies will be taking the necessary steps to be sure their annuity contracts and custodial accounts reflect the availability of features subject to the rules under the written plan. In the past, such language has not been an issue but, going forward, it is important that those changes be made.

Types of 403(b) Contributions Permitted; Limits and Coordination with 457(b) Plans

VOLUNTARY SALARY REDUCTION CONTRIBUTIONS

Employees are permitted to elect to reduce salary and to direct those salary reduction contributions to providers that are offered in the employer's plan.

Voluntary salary reduction contributions are referred to in the code as "elective deferrals" governed by the limits set out in Section 402(g). Elective deferrals include deferrals to a tax-sheltered annuity, a 401(k) plan, Salary Reduction Simplified Employee Pension (SARSEP), and a Simple IRA or Simple 401(k). The total amount of elective deferrals to any or all of those plans cannot exceed the limits in effect for the specific affected income tax year, regardless of the number of plans or employers with which the taxpayer makes those deferrals. Contributions to a Section 501(c)(18) plan, which are the grandfathered pre-403(b) salary reduction plans that were once available, will also directly offset other elective deferrals; however, those plans are rarely seen.

Elective Deferrals Made Pretax

Elective deferrals can be made on a pretax basis in which federal income taxes and, where applicable, state income taxes are not withheld or due on those deferrals until distributions occur. The income taxes are also deferred on the earnings or growth in the account until such time as the values are distributed. At distribution, ordinary income taxes must be paid on the amounts distributed. Social Security, Medicare, and other payroll taxes will apply at the time contributions are made.

Elective Deferrals Made after Tax to the Roth 403(b)

Effective January 1, 2006, elective deferrals can also be made after tax to the Roth 403(b). Federal income taxes and, where applicable, state income taxes must be withheld on the Roth 403(b) contributions. Participants who satisfy both the five-year holding period (measured from the first tax year in which a Roth 403(b) contribution is made through the employer, or the first tax year of another Roth 403(b) or Roth 401(k) account rolled into the current employer's account) and one of three qualifying events (age 59½, death, or disability) will receive all distributions income tax–free. Social Security, Medicare, and other payroll taxes will apply at the time contributions are made. A growing number of employers have added, or plan to add, the Roth 403(b) option as long as the product providers agree to separately account for those contributions.

Contribution Limits

Contribution calculations for a 403(b) plan are relatively simple for both the basic limit and the age 50+ catch-up contribution, since the maximum available amount is based upon the lesser of the Section 415(c) limit (100 percent of includable compensation capped at $51,000 in 2013 and indexed in $1,000 increments), as explained later in this chapter. The employee's voluntary salary reduction contributions are further limited under Section 402(g). The following list provides the limits for the past several years for 403(b), 401(k), and grandfathered SARSEP plans:

Year	Amount
2005	$14,000
2006	$15,000
2007, 2008	$15,500
2009, 2010, 2011	$16,500
2012	$17,000
2013	$17,500

Indexed in $500 increments, generally posted by the IRS in late October of each year. Whether elective deferrals are made pretax or after tax to the Roth 403(b), or both, the single limit applies in combination.

Age 50+ Catch-Up Contribution

Code Section IRC 414(v) permits employees who will be age 50 or older by the end of the affected income tax year to contribute extra amounts as follows:

Year	Amount
2005	$4,000
2006	$5,000
2007	$5,000
2008	$5,000
2009–2013	$5,500

Indexed in $500 increments and posted in late October of each year by the IRS.

The new catch-up contribution does not affect any other limit—it is, quite simply, a catch-up opportunity with only two conditions: (1) that the participant be at least age 50 before the end of the affected year, and (2) that the participant have enough includable compensation to support the contribution.

Fifteen-Years-of-Service Increase

Additionally, Section 402(g)(7) provides that participants in the 403(b) plan only may be eligible to contribute as much as an extra $3,000 more than the basic limit if:

- they have fifteen or more years of service with the current employer, and
- they have not contributed on average $5,000 or more to elective deferral plans of the current employer in years prior to the current one, and
- they have not previously used $15,000 in the increased limit with the current employer.

Both the age 50+ catch-up and the fifteen-years-of-service increased limit can be used in the same year; however, the fifteen-years-of-service limit should be used first. (As an example, an employee who is eligible to use both catch-ups could not choose to use the age 50+ catch-up and save the fifteen-years-of-service increase for a later date. Employees eligible for both catch-ups who exceed the basic limits are considered first to be using the fifteen-years-of-service limit.)

Payroll Taxes/Tax Reporting

Payroll taxes, including FICA, where applicable, do apply to any salary reduction contribution (whether voluntary or mandatory) to a 403(b) plan. Salary reduction contributions are reported on each participating employee's W-2 tax form issued after the tax year. The instructions to the W-2 include a code specific to the pretax 403(b) contribution and a code specific to the Roth 403(b) contribution.

EMPLOYER CONTRIBUTIONS

Public education employers are not subject to the nondiscrimination rules for employer (nonsalary reduction) contributions to a 403(b) plan and are additionally exempt from Title I of ERISA. For that reason, many school business officials have taken the necessary steps to selectively make those contributions (as explained in chapter 13).

Additionally, the 403(b) written plan must include language that permits employer contributions (which can be made on a discretionary basis) to the 403(b) plan. Such contributions, which can be made both during years of service and for up to five years after service is terminated, are being effectively used for budget-saving measures, since there are no payroll taxes on contributions to retirement plans.

Postretirement Contributions Explained

It is permissible for the employer to make contributions for a period of up to five tax years following the year that employees terminate service with the employer. Thus, employers can establish early retirement incentive programs or replace more expensive unused vacation and sick leave pay with postretirement contributions to a 403(b) plan. Section 403(b)(3), which is the definition of includable compensation specific only to a 403(b) plan, was amended effective January 1, 2002, to permit that unique treatment. The final 403(b) regulations make it clear that contributions cannot continue to be made following the month of the recipient participant's death.

This has a considerable impact on helping reduce and manage school district budgets.

Limits for Employer Contributions

The Section 415(c) limit is the only limit applicable to employer contributions to a 403(b) plan. That limit is the lesser of 100 percent of includable compensation or $51,000 in 2013. It is indexed in $1,000 increments and, as previously mentioned, the indexed increases in retirement plan limits are announced after the end of the third calendar quarter each year.

The Section 415(c) limit applies to the combination of the employer contributions to the 403(b) plan, the salary reduction contribution to the plan, and the age 50+ catch-up contribution. For example, an employee, who has includable compensation of over $51,000 in 2013, is making salary reduction contributions of $17,500, plus an additional $5,500 utilizing the age 50+ catch-up contribution. The employer is permitted to contribute $51,000 minus $17,500, or $33,500, to the 403(b) plan. The $5,500 age 50+ catch-up contribution does not affect the $51,000 limit. Thus, the total amount that can be contributed in 2013 is $56,500—$23,000 by the age 50+ employee and $33,500 by the employer. In 2013, the limits then applicable permitted a total contribution of $56,500 by the employer and the age 50+ employees.

As the limits change due to indexing, the employer's third-party plan administrator and/or the product providers will notify the payroll personnel of any limit changes for the subsequent tax year.

Payroll Taxes/Fringe Benefits/Tax Reporting

Employer contributions to a 403(b) plan are not subject to payroll taxes and, in most states, fringe benefits. Thus, an employer contribution is much less expensive than compensation and can represent a significant savings for school districts.

Employer contributions to a 403(b) plan are not reported on the employees' W-2 tax forms since they are not part of the payroll process.

COMPENSATION DEFINITION

The definition for includable compensation (Section 403(b)(3)) applicable to a 403(b) plan is unique—it does not apply to any other type of retirement plan. To determine eligible contribution limits, the compensation earned in the most recent period that adds up to one full twelve-month period of service (through the end of the current tax year) minus any mandatory pretax contributions made to the state retirement system defined benefit or defined contribution plan is used. Thus, includable compensation may include compensation earned in multiple income tax years. For example, a part-time employee would be permitted to use compensation earned in as many tax years as are needed to be equivalent to one full twelve-month period of service. An employee terminating service in midyear will use compensation earned in both the previous and the current year. Keep in mind that includable compensation will not include amounts earned in prior years (such as unused sick leave or vacation pay). The definition is particularly important in establishing the eligibility to make contributions on behalf of employees who have terminated employment (as explained in this chapter and expanded in chapter 13).

An employer who wishes to make early retirement incentive contributions or employer contributions in lieu of severance pay bases those contributions on the amount of includable compensation earned in the last full twelve-month period of service. For example, if the affected employee has more than $51,000 in includable compensation (the dollar limit under Section 415(c) in 2013) in the last twelve-month period of service, the employer is then permitted to make postemployment contributions for each of up to five tax years after the tax year of the employee's severance of employment in the amount of $51,000 (indexed in $1,000 increments). This will mean that as much as $255,000 can be contributed (for example, to buy out the contract of a key employee or to replace large amounts of unused sick leave and vacation pay for retiring administrators).

COORDINATING 403(b) AND 457(b) CONTRIBUTIONS

Employees can contribute the maximum permissible amount to both the employer's 403(b) plan and the 457(b) plan. In 2013, 457(b) contribution limits were $17,500 under the basic limit, plus $5,500 for those participants age 50+. Thus, an employee needing to maximize retirement or deferred compensation plan opportunities could, as long as he or she has sufficient compensation, contribute $46,000 to the two plans—$23,000 each.

Note that 457(b) plans also permit a final three-year catch-up contribution if there is unused limit available. That special catch-up contribution, explained in depth in chapter 16, is complex and should not be permitted without a calculation done by professionals.

12

Avoiding Violation of the Universal Availability Requirement

Because the final regulations make it clear that a failure to meet the requirements of the universal availability rules is a plan disqualification event, it is important that employers take steps to avoid the violation. Many believe (as will be further explained) that the simplest method of ensuring compliance is to make the plan available to all common-law employees who will contribute $200 or more each year. This avoids an inadvertent violation (in particular, violations based on excluding employees that work part time) and likely does not increase administrative burdens for employers, since most very part-time individuals will not choose to participate.

Section 403(b)(12)(ii) provides that if any employee is given the right to participate in the voluntary tax-sheltered annuity plan, then virtually every employee must be given that same right. The only employees who can be excluded from the voluntary plan are the following:

- Employees who will contribute $200 or less per year. (It will be important that at least one of the service providers agree to accept contributions as small as $200 per year. Many will agree to do so, even though the normal minimum requirements of the provider may be more than $200 per year.)
- Employees who will normally work less than twenty hours per week. The final regulations apply a safe harbor standard in which employers can utilize one thousand hours per year to determine whether employees can be excluded. In the year of hire, if a employee is reasonably expected to work one thousand or more hours, that employee cannot be excluded. After the year of hire,

the employer can look back to the previous year to determine hours worked.

- Employees who participate in another voluntary salary reduction plan such as the 457(b) plan or a 401(k) plan (if applicable).
- Students performing services described in Section 3121(b)(1).
- Nonresident aliens with no U.S. source income.

Caution: The IRS takes the position that if any employee in an excluded class of employees is permitted to participate, then every employee in that class must also be permitted to do so.

Because violation of the universal eligibility rule is the second most common violation and potentially one of the most costly violations, employers are encouraged to permit virtually every employee who will contribute more than $200 per year to participate if they wish to do so. This should include substitute teachers if there is a work history of service that might add up to twenty or more hours per week. In including substitute teachers or other employees with uncertain work schedules, the employer could require that contributions be made only on a percentage of salary basis to avoid the possible problem of an employee not having a paycheck each pay period.

The final regulations also require that, no less than once a year, every eligible employee be given a meaningful opportunity to participate. Obviously a meaningful opportunity must include notice of their rights and the conditions under which they are permitted to participate. New reports of IRS audits and an interview with a senior staff specialist from the Audit Division of the IRS provide some direction on the meaning of "meaningful opportunity," which the IRS has verbally indicated is being referred to as "effective opportunity." The IRS field examiner, at the time the employer is selected for audit, is looking at the rate of participation in the plan. According to reports, and the IRS senior staff specialist, if participation is low (reportedly in the 18–20 percent range in 2013 audits), the field examiner is asking the employers to share their employee educational program with the examiner. According to the senior staff specialist, providing an effective opportunity to enroll or make changes will be effective if diverse methods are used. An example of an educational program with which product providers and third-party administrators can help would include those listed below:

- Frequent employee educational seminars (some of the providers offer financial literacy seminars covering all of the sources of retirement income, including Social Security and state retirement system benefits). School business officials, or another key staff member, should begin the seminars with introductory remarks signaling the employer's support of voluntary savings programs for employees. The presenting providers must be required to share with employees a list of all approved providers in the plan along with contact information for each provider.
- Online retirement planning tools for employees that have access to and knowledge of utilization of online tools. According to the Census Bureau, some 30 percent of consumers either do not have computers or do not have Internet service; thus the online tools should be only one of the educational methods offered.
- Face-to-face financial advisors to meet individually with employees, both to motivate them to initially enroll and to continue and increase contributions over time. Numerous studies reveal that not only do a large percentage of employees need the services of face-to-face advisors, but those using advisors will also contribute more over time and have more diversified investments.

Additionally, to ensure compliance with the meaningful opportunity to participate, frequent ability to enroll or make changes would provide a more effective result.

Increasing participation rates will benefit both the employer (giving employees the ability to retire at normal retirement ages will save budget dollars) and the employees (satisfaction with the employer-sponsored plan results in greater appreciation of the plan).

13

Employer Contributions

There are no nondiscrimination rules applicable to nonelective (employer) contributions to a public education–sponsored 403(b) plan. Section 403(b)(12)(C) specifically exempts any governmental employer from the limitations imposed by those rules. Additionally, because the retirement plans sponsored by governmental employers are specifically exempted from the requirements of Title I of ERISA, there are no barriers to selectively making employer contributions for certain employees.

School districts and community colleges are routinely developing administrative policies that direct employer contributions to their 403(b) plan to do the following:

- Incentivize early retirement of certain employees. Under the post-EGTRRA rules, the likelihood is that early retirement incentives will focus on employer contributions made postretirement.
- Replace severance pay with employer contributions.
- Recruit and retain specialty teachers or key employees.
- Buy out the individually negotiated contracts of certain employees such as the superintendent of schools.
- Reduce the unfunded liabilities of unused leave pay accruals by replacing some of those accruals with employer contributions.

While nondiscrimination rules are not an issue, it will be important for school business officials to include language in the written plan that permits employer contributions on a discretionary basis. The sample plan document (available at www.asbointl.org) includes an adoption agreement in which the employer has the flexibility to include employer contributions (on a discretionary basis, to be utilized as desired), and the sample language in that document supports the making of employer contributions. The IRS-approved document language should also include employer contributions, which can be implemented as the employer wishes. Additionally, the employer will want to construct administrative language that will describe the employer contribution plan in a manner that does not give affected employees an option of receiving either an employer contribution or compensation.

If an option is provided, the employer contribution will be considered an elective deferral, subject to payroll taxes and the lower elective deferral limit. (Sample language can be provided to the employer's legal counsel with contact to this author.) Additionally, if those disputed contributions are made postemployment, they would be disallowed by the IRS because elective deferrals are not permitted after the employee severs employment (except for certain types of severance pay paid no later than the end of the calendar year of severance, or, if later, within two and a half months after employment ceases, as explained in chapter 11).

Employers interested in establishing employer contribution plans should review chapter 11 for the permitted limits (for the 2013 tax year, as indexed) and check both state and local laws, as well as any union collective bargaining agreements and individually negotiated contracts, to be certain there are no barriers to the arrangements.

14

Communicating with Your Employees

Because the final 403(b) regulations present significant changes for the employees that do, or will, participate in the 403(b) plan, it is important to communicate with them as the employer works diligently to maintain compliance with standards that did not exist before. It is also important to keep the union representatives of those employees informed to ward off any potential issues.

Remember that employees who participate in 403(b) plans are also impacted by the final 403(b) regulations with the loss of control of their accounts, formerly an important aspect of a 403(b) plan. Additionally, when they need such transactions as loans or hardship withdrawals, they may need to meet new, more stringent requirements, which may delay the processing time for them. Finally, they no longer have the freedom to choose any 403(b) investment option they wish—they are limited now only to the options that you have made available to them in the 403(b) plan.

Key to a good communication program will be an ongoing effort to keep employees and unions in the loop with frequent communications about any changes to the plans in the future. Keep in mind that a good communication program can also respond to the requirement that employees be given a meaningful or effective notice of the right to participate in the voluntary plan.

This chapter focuses on suggestions to aid employers in maintaining a good relationship with the employees who are enjoying the benefit of accumulating retirement savings to keep the level of satisfaction at the maximum level:

- The appointment of a committee that includes rank-and-file employees and/or union representatives to help construct a good communications plan will help employers with input.
- In each communication, it makes sense to continue to remind employees that the employer's efforts to comply with final regulations are done to protect the tax status of each participant's account.
- From time to time (certainly in the required annual meaningful notice of the right to participate), employers should remind employees of the features included in the plan. For example, is the Roth 403(b) option available?
- It is inevitable that there will be occasional breakdowns in service or glitches that develop, which could slow down response time to participants' requests for transactions. Assurances to employees (and explanations of why such events occurred) that these matters are being addressed on an ongoing basis will help ward off dissatisfaction.
- The final approved providers (those that receive contributions on and after January 1, 2009, must be included in the written plan regardless of whether it is adopted before January 1, 2009, or, if later, before December 31, 2009) may change over time. Perhaps one or more of the approved providers will not be able to continue to accommodate the new requirements and may choose to relinquish the payroll slot—or perhaps one or more of the providers will violate the terms of a service provider agreement and need to be dropped. Communication with impacted employees is vital.
- Over time, employers may, through employee demand, wish to add one or more providers (either to replace deselected providers or simply to offer choices not included by the other providers). Communicating the addition of providers is not only important but also a goodwill gesture.

Various methods can be used to regularly communicate; however, perhaps a regular "All About Your 403(b) Plan" column in the district's newsletter would aid in the ease of communication. Ask your third-party plan administrator or your product providers for examples of employee communications to help guide you to a more successful plan.

Remember that, as an employer, you have taken careful and time-consuming steps to offer this important benefit to your employees— and communication will be key to helping your employees appreciate that effort.

IRS Audits, Corrections, and Compliance Projects

It is important to note that, according to reports of IRS audit results in public schools, not a single 403(b) plan has been disqualified; however, with the requirements under the final regulations, it is clear that there are three specific plan defects that are listed as "plan disqualification events." Those are as follows:

- Failure to adopt a written plan and operate under the terms of that written plan
- Violation of the universal availability requirements (covered in chapter 12)
- An ineligible employer (one that has adopted a 403(b) plan, but is not either a public education or a 501(c)(3) employer)

All other plan defects are operational failures, and, while operational failures would have a negative effect on the accounts of employees incurring the defect (such as violation of the loan limits), there would be no negative impact on all of the other participants' accounts.

THE TWO MOST COMMON VIOLATIONS

1. Uncorrected contributions made in excess of the eligible limits. Now that the pre-EGTRRA exclusion allowance has been permanently repealed, the primary cause of excess contributions is the increased limit for employees who have fifteen or more years of service. As explained in chapter 11, this catch-up contribution

should not be permitted without a required calculation from your third-party plan administrator or your product providers. It makes sense for your payroll staff to build the basic limit for each tax year into their system, so that any contributions in excess of the basic limit trigger a request for a calculation, which should be maintained in payroll records (in the event of a need to correct an excess contribution, or to respond to the questions of the IRS in the event of an audit).

2. Violation of the universal availability nondiscrimination rule. The second most common violation is one for which employers must assume responsibility. In general, the requirement is that if any employee is given the opportunity to participate in the 403(b) plan, then virtually every employee must be allowed to participate. The primary problem in public schools has been the exclusion of substitute teachers and employees who want to contribute minimal amounts. The nondiscrimination rule and recommended approaches to avoid the violation are covered in depth in chapter 12.

NEW IRS INTEREST

Loans and Hardship Withdrawals

The Internal Revenue Service now requires that the employer assume responsibility for compliance with loan rules, and the rules for hardship withdrawals, including the suspension of salary reduction contributions to all voluntary plans of the employer for a period of six months (under the Safe Harbor rules). This is one of the problem areas found in audits prior to the January 1, 2009, effective date of the final regulations, and it will continue to be an audit focus going forward.

Failure to Adopt and Conform to the Written Plan

This has become a focus of IRS audits of tax years 2010 and later. And, since failure to adopt a written plan is a violation that could be a plan disqualification event, it is vital that all employers meet the requirement.

IRS COMPLIANCE PROJECTS

A recent development stems from the formation of the Employee Plans Compliance Unit and the selection of projects applicable to 403(b) plans. As many readers know, the IRS can (and does) select specific projects that result in letters and questionnaires sent to public school districts across the country. The first of the 403(b)-related compliance projects involved the mailing of letters to districts in all states (completed in early 2009), checking to see if employers were meeting the requirements of the universal availability nondiscrimination rules. There has been discussion that a similar project may involve the sending of letters to employers to confirm that a written plan is in place—additionally, the IRS has announced that there will be follow-up letters to employers to check that correction has been made to previously disclosed universal availability problems identified in the first series of letters and questionnaires. In general, the IRS has required that the employer make nonelective contributions to all employees improperly excluded from the plan, for all of the years those employees were excluded, to correct the violation.

Thus, even if audits are not taking place, employers should be sure to comply with the requirements under the 403(b) code and the final 403(b) regulations, since defects could surface through ongoing compliance projects.

CORRECTION OF PLAN DEFECTS

Periodically, the IRS posts an updated revenue procedure to describe correction programs available for 403(b) and other types of plans. The latest version at press time is Revenue Procedure 2013-12, posted in 2013. In that procedure appear the processes and procedures and the correction mechanisms available for correction of all manner of defects. The new revenue procedure, for the first time, permits correction of the failure to adopt a written plan by December 31, 2009, with the filing of a formal submission under the Voluntary Correction Program (VCP). Any employer considering utilizing one of the available correction procedures should check for the latest version of the procedures. In the meantime, there are three correction processes available:

1. Self-Correction Program (SCP), under which only operational failures can be corrected (most commonly used to correct excess contributions, as explained below). The employer simply corrects the operational failure when it is discovered. No formal submission, penalties, or fees apply to self-correction. Note that insignificant failures can be corrected at any time; however, significant failures must be corrected within two plan years of their occurrence. It is not entirely clear what is considered significant; however, presumably that would be defects that are widespread.

2. VCP. This is available to correct any and all types of failures (such as eligibility failures) but does require the preparation of a detailed formal submission with the payment of a submission fee. Note that an eligibility failure would include not only an employer who is not eligible to sponsor a 403(b) plan at all, but also the inclusion of ineligible investment options (such as the use of mutual funds without a custodial account, or a self-directed brokerage account in which stocks and bonds are traded). Because a submission under VCP is an extensive process, it is highly recommended that any employer utilizing this correction procedure retain legal assistance or the assistance of another professional such as an IRS-enrolled agent.

3. Audit Closing Agreement Program (CAP). The final correction procedure is nothing more than a negotiated settlement with the IRS to correct defects following an audit. Audit CAP permits the employer to potentially be granted the right to correct such defects in a manner that reduces possible sanctions.

Correcting Excess Contributions

Excess contributions will not cause the entire TSA plan to be disqualified—in general, only the affected participant's 403(b) account or a portion of that account will lose its status. This differs from a 457(b) plan, in which excess contributions that are not corrected could, indeed, cause disqualification of the entire plan.

The IRS focuses on excesses due to use of the fifteen-years-of-service increased elective deferral limit, contributions to multiple elective deferral plans such as 403(b) and 401(k), and combined employer and employee contributions that have caused the IRC 415(c) limit to be exceeded.

Excess Deferrals

An excess deferral is a contribution that exceeds the Section 402(g) limits (note that those limits are covered thoroughly in chapter 11). The increased limit for eligible employees with fifteen or more years of service may permit up to an additional $3,000 in elective deferrals if a calculation indicates eligibility to use that increase.

Section 402(g) provides that an excess deferral can be corrected at the participant's request through distribution, provided that distribution of both the excess and its earnings is made by April 15 of the calendar year following the excess. The service provider will distribute the excess and issue the proper income tax reporting form. The affected participant will pay the income taxes on the excess deferral for the year in which it was made, and on the earnings for the year of distribution.

If the excess deferral is not distributed by April 15 following the year of the excess, the participant is not permitted to correct the excess through distribution. However, the employer can, under SCP, request that the excess amount be reported as taxable. The provider will issue a Form 1099R. Note that an excess not corrected in a timely way will result in double taxation to the participant (it would be taxed once for the year in which the excess occurred, and again in the year distributed). The employer should cite the self-correction procedure in the request for tax reporting of the excess amount, then retain the correction in the records in the event of an audit.

EXCESSES IN THE SECTION 415(c) LIMIT

In years before 2002, the 415(c) limit was 25 percent of includable compensation with a $35,000 limit in 2001. Since the Section 415(c) limit has been greatly simplified (the lesser of 100 percent of includable compensation or $51,000 in 2013, as indexed), there should not be a great many 415(c) excesses. Refer to the detailed explanation of this limit (and the other applicable limits) in chapter 11.

If that limit is exceeded, the final regulations require that an uncorrected excess be set aside in a taxable (Section 403(c)) account. Employers should take care to get agreement (in the Investment Provider Service Agreement, a sample of which appears in chapter 19) from the providers that they will meet the segregation requirement and that the amount set aside is properly reported.

16

The Basics of Governmental 457(b) Plans

This chapter provides a brief description of 457(b) governmental plans, since so many public school and community college employers have added or plan to add those plans as a part of the employee benefits package. Please be aware that this is intended to be a basic description and that only governmental 457(b) plans are being addressed. The 457(b) plans sponsored by 501(c) tax-exempt organizations (that are not also governmental in nature) have substantial differences.

The growing interest in the establishment of a 457(b) plan by public education employers is due to the EGTRRA changes. Now that the contributions to a 457(b) plan and a 403(b) plan are not required to be coordinated, many public education employers want to make the new double deferral opportunities available to the employees who need the additional way to accumulate retirement savings (and defer current income taxes). Also, 457(b) plans appeal to employees who plan to work for a period of years, and then leave to pursue other endeavors. The fact that there is not a 10 percent penalty tax on distributions will mean that the saved 457(b) plan values can be used for immediate needs once employment is severed.

DIFFERENCES BETWEEN 457(b) PLANS AND 403(b) PLANS

In a 403(b) plan the employer is not required to maintain any ownership in the account; however, in a governmental 457(b) plan, the employer is required to own the 457(b) asset for the benefit of the participant and beneficiaries. Other differences between the two types of plans include:

- In-service distributions from a 457(b) plan are permitted only at age 70½* or upon confirmation of an unexpected emergency that creates hardship. In a 403(b) plan, in-service distributions are permitted at age 59½, or upon a more relaxed standard for hardship withdrawals.
- Distributions from a 457(b) plan are not subject to an IRS-assessed penalty tax, while pre-59½ distributions from a 403(b) plan may be subject to a 10 percent penalty tax.
- Generally, state statutes may apply specific fiduciary standards or requirements to 457(b) governmental plans, while, generally, those same requirements may not apply to 403(b) plans.
- Investment options in a 457(b) plan are not limited to annuities or mutual funds held in custodial accounts as they are in a 403(b) plan.
- Employer contributions to a 457(b) plan are subject to the lower salary reduction contribution limits and to payroll taxes, while such contributions to a 403(b) plan have higher limits and payroll taxes do not apply.
- There is no universal availability requirement in a 457(b) plan, while that requirement (see chapter 12) does apply to a 403(b) plan (except for churches and certain church organizations).
- A Roth option can now be offered in 457(b) plans.
- The fifteen-years-of-service catch-up available in a 403(b) plan is not permitted in 457(b) plans; however, there is a catch-up option (if permitted in the plan) that may be used in the final three years prior to normal retirement age, as listed in the plan.

SIMILARITIES BETWEEN 457(b) GOVERNMENTAL AND 403(b) PLANS

- Both plans require a written plan document, and both plans permit the employer to select optional features (such as loans or hardship withdrawals). Most of the providers that offer 457(b) governmen-

---

* There is a limited exception for certain accounts holding less than $5,000 in assets.

tal plans have specimen plan documents available. Additionally, the IRS has issued suggested plan document language.

- Both plans require that the employer assume compliance responsibility (however, both plans permit the employer to delegate the transactions necessary to meet compliance requirements to third parties). As is true of 403(b) plans, such responsibilities can be delegated to the product providers or a TPA.
- The basic salary reduction contributions are identical in the two plans.
- Both governmental 457(b) and 403(b) plans permit the age 50+ catch-up contribution.

Contribution Limits

The Section 415(c) limit of the lesser of 100 percent of includable compensation or $51,000 (in 2013, as indexed) does not apply to a 457(b) plan as it does to a 403(b) plan. The contribution limits for 457(b) governmental plans are as follows:

Year	Basic Limit	Age 50+ Catch-Up Contribution	Final Three-Year Catch-Up
2006	$15,000	$5,000	$30,000
2007, 2008	$15,500	$5,000	$31,000
2009–2011	$16,500	$5,500	$33,000
2012	$17,000	$5,500	$34,000
2013	$17,500	$5,500	$36,000

Note that the basic limit and the age 50+ catch-up contribution limit are exactly the same as voluntary salary reduction contributions to the 403(b) arrangement, as explained in chapter 11.

As a reminder, note that the final three-year option is a complex limit that will require a calculation. A few basic requirements applicable to that limit are as follows:

- It is available only in one, two, or three of the years before the year in which "normal retirement age" occurs, as defined in the plan document.

- It is available only to the extent of any "underutilized limitation" during the years the affected participant was eligible to participate in the 457(b) plan. Thus, if the employer's 457(b) plan is being installed and made available to employees for the first time, there is no underutilized limitation.
- For years before 2002, voluntary salary reduction contributions made by the affected employee to all plans of any employer are counted against the 457(b) limit. Thus, for example, employees who have routinely contributed to their 403(b) plan must count those contributions for purposes of determining underutilized limits.

Because excess contributions due to improper use of the final three-year catch-up are reportedly common, employers should never permit this option without a calculation.

Coordination of the Two Catch-Up Options

Employees who are both age 50+ and eligible to use the final three-year catch-up option are not permitted to use both in the same year. The final regulations for 457(b) plans provide that only the catch-up option that permits the greater limit can be used.

Salary Reduction Agreements

In a 457(b) plan, the code requires that the salary reduction agreement must be received before the first of the month in which salary reduction contributions will be made (with the exception of newly hired employees, if certain conditions are met). This rule does not apply to a 403(b) arrangement.

Plan Assets

While the plan assets are owned by the employer (until distributed), it is important to note that they are owned "for the benefit of the participant or beneficiaries" and are required to be set aside in trust, or in an annuity contract or custodial account that is qualified to accept 457(b) contributions. The assets are protected through that "set aside" from the general creditors of the employer.

Investment Options

In a 403(b) arrangement, investment options are limited to 403(b)(1) annuities or 403(b)(7) custodial accounts in which domestically traded mutual funds can be offered. There is no such limitation in a 457(b) plan, which can include stocks and bonds, bank or credit union savings accounts, and annuities and mutual funds.

Employer Contributions

Employer contributions to a 403(b) plan are subject to a higher limit than are voluntary salary reduction contributions (e.g., $51,000 in 2013), while 457(b) employer contributions are subject to the same lower limit as are salary reduction contributions.

The limit (listed under Contribution Limits) applies to the combination of employer contributions and employee salary reduction contributions to the 457(b) plan. Additionally, in a 403(b) plan, employer (nonelective) contributions are not subject to payroll taxes such as FICA—in a 457(b) plan, those contributions are subject to payroll taxes. For those reasons, we rarely see employer contributions made (in the public education segment) to a 457(b) plan.

IRS Premature Distribution Tax

In a 403(b) arrangement (and other types of retirement plans or IRAs), a 10 percent penalty tax may apply to withdrawals made before age 59½. In a 457(b) plan, there is no IRS premature distribution penalty tax for withdrawals at any age.

In-Service Withdrawals

The ability for participants to make in-service withdrawals from a 457(b) plan is more restricted than in a 403(b) plan. Withdrawals can be made during employment only in the following situations:

- At age 70½ (in a 403(b), withdrawals are permitted at age 59½)
- Account values under $5,000 with no contributions made for two years prior to the withdrawal (assuming the employer's plan permits this feature)

- Emergency hardship (generally an unexpected emergency event), unlike the more lenient hardship withdrawal rules for a 403(b) plan

Loans

In a 403(b) plan, the loan requirements are covered in IRC 72(p) and subsequent regulations issued by the Internal Revenue Service. In a 457(b) governmental plan, loans are also governed by IRC 72(p) and subsequent regulations; however, the final regulations for 457(b) plans also discuss a facts-and-circumstances standard for loans. Those final regulations, issued in 2003, state, in part, "the determination of whether the availability of the loan, or a failure to repay the loan is in any . . . respect a violation of the requirements of section 457(b) and the regulations, depends on the facts and circumstances." Among those standards are whether the interest rate being charged is reasonable, whether there are repayment safeguards that a "prudent lender" would apply, and whether loans are available to all participants on a "reasonably equivalent" basis. These standards are somewhat similar to the standards that are applied to loans from ERISA plans; thus, employers who plan to permit loans in their 457(b) plans will want to be certain that the loan provisions do follow the final regulations.

COMPLIANCE AND CORRECTION ISSUES FOR 457(b) GOVERNMENTAL PLANS

Audits of 457(b) Plans

The IRS has reported that audits of 457(b) plans are under way; however, examination guidelines (which serve as a road map of approaches taken in audits) have not yet been issued. Reports of audit results tell us that the most common violations are excess contributions and failure to set aside the assets to protect them from the general creditors of the employer, as further explained and expanded below.

Defects Found in Audits

In recent reports of audits of 457(b) plans, we have learned that some of the violations discovered in the few reported are as follows:

- Employer contributions to the plan that mistakenly utilized the $51,000 limit (which limit is applicable only to 403(b), 401(k), and other defined contribution plans), thus causing excess contributions
- Excess contributions due to use of the final three-year catch-up option (either because the participant used the option in years other than the last three years before normal retirement age in the plan or because the option was used when there was no underutilized limit available)

Correction Procedures

While 457(b) plans have not yet formally been included in the IRS revenue procedures that cover correction procedures for 403(b) plans, qualified plans, and Simplified Employee Pension Plans, the most current version of those procedures (Revenue Procedure 2013-12) indicates that correction procedures can be based on the same principles. Additionally, the final 457(b) regulations that were issued in 2003 do provide some guidance on the correction of excess contributions. Based on those final regulations, the public education or other governmental employer can request distribution of excess contributions "as soon as practicable following discovery of the excess." The 457(b) plan vendors would make those distributions (only at the employer's request) to each affected participant and issue an IRS Form 1099R reporting the distributions as taxable.

If the excess contributions that occurred in the employer's 457(b) plans are not corrected as soon as practical after discovery, the final regulations state that the 457(b) plan becomes an ineligible plan (meaning that all plan assets will become taxable). If there are excess contributions to this employer's plan due to an employee's participation in another employer's 457(b) plan, it is important to note that failure to correct those excesses would not disqualify the 457(b) plan.

17

403(b) Compliance Checklist

The checklist is provided as an additional tool for school personnel who are implementing, adjusting, or operating under the terms of the compliance procedures as required in the final 403(b) regulations. Those items in boldface print are included to help clarify meanings of certain aspects of the checklist.

EMPLOYER RESPONSIBILITIES

❏ If your current written plan does not include update services, be alert to any need to amend the document (due to additional regulation or legislation). Consider adoption of an IRS-approved plan document at the time they become available.

❏ Monitor your universal availability requirements carefully to ensure that all eligible employees are given not only a meaningful opportunity to participate but also a meaningful notice (at least annually) of their right to do so.

- If you have chosen to exclude employees normally not working one thousand hours per year, establish a tracking system of hours worked so that no eligible employee is inadvertently excluded.

- Be prepared, if you have excluded those employees, to open up eligibility to all part-time employees if any one employee working less than the safe harbor hours is permitted to be included.

- Be aware that the IRS is looking carefully at the issue of meaningful opportunity to participate when participation rates are low (see chapter 12).

❏ Develop procedures to monitor and deal with the product and investment providers to be sure they are complying with the terms of the written plan and have executed service provider agreements in order to be included as an approved provider in the written plan.

❏ Be prepared to deselect any providers that cannot or will not meet those requirements.

Points: If you are using a third-party plan administrator (TPA), you can delegate the monitoring process to that TPA. If you are partnering with the product and investment providers, you may want to appoint an oversight committee (include someone from your payroll department, since those individuals will be dealing with the daily operation of the 403(b) plan) to assist with this process. If providers are deselected, allow ample time to notify the employees participating with those providers so that they can select from the remaining list of approved providers. Be sure that any deselected providers will continue to share information on the accounts they held prior to deselection.

❏ Develop procedures to add product and investment providers, including the execution of the proper service provider agreements and addition of new providers to the list of approved providers included on the addendum to your written plan.

Over time, some of the providers originally selected may need to be deselected, or may choose to exit your plan, or your original product selection may not have included a variety of choices to satisfy the goals and needs of your employees.

❏ Prepare ongoing communications with employees about the compliance activities that may impact them, and also to remind employees from time to time of the features included in your plan. Note that such communications could be incorporated into the meaningful notice of their right to participate.

Be sure to emphasize that the activities are undertaken to protect the qualified tax status of their 403(b) accounts. If there has been a slowdown in response time for transactions (such as distributions or loans), help them understand that the processes that are in place are required in order to be sure eligibility requirements are met. It may make sense to appoint an employee and union representatives committee to provide input into the communication process.

❏ Require that your investment and product providers notify any financial advisors contracted with them to work with your employees of the specific features included in your plan.
   • Sending a copy of the adoption agreement used to select those features with the request should avoid any misunderstandings.
❏ Establish reasonable solicitation rules outlining the conditions under which product providers can see your employees on site, and be sure that information has been communicated to the providers. Note that the service provider agreement in chapter 19 requires that the provider meet the rules (but you must communicate those rules to those providers).

Point: The rules should make clear that the representatives cannot interrupt the normal workday of employees; rather, contacts can be made only before or after classroom instruction or during lunch hours.

❏ Include in the employee communications a copy of the solicitation rules.
❏ Require that the providers distribute copies of the solicitation rules to their agents and/or employees.
❏ Notify noncooperative service providers that their payroll privileges have been terminated or amended in accordance with the procedures finalized during the preparation period.
❏ Notify affected employees that they must redirect their ongoing contributions to a cooperative service provider.
   • Provide a period of time for the employee to make the change.

• Provide a list of the approved providers from which the employee can select a new provider.

SYSTEMS AND ADMINISTRATION

❏ Set the basic elective deferral limits as the maximum acceptable amount without calculations. Be sure to amend that limit, as indexing causes it to increase (limits for the following year are announced late each October).

Point: The system should reject any contributions that will exceed the basic IRC 402(g) limit for the applicable year, unless calculations in support of use of one of the catch-up contributions are submitted with the salary reduction agreement.

❏ As the elective deferral limits increase, update your salary reduction agreement. Note that the sample agreement in chapter 19 includes the annual limits for 2013 and will need to be changed each time the limits change.

❏ Maintain copies of the following:
   1. The current salary reduction agreement for each participant
   2. Any communications to employees intended to fulfill the meaningful notice requirement
   3. Service provider agreements
   4. Any communication to the providers

❏ Receive agreement from your product and investment providers, or your TPA (if any), that all data necessary to meet the requests of an IRS field examiner conducting an audit can be quickly provided to you.

This will include records of outstanding loans, hardship or other distributions, whether required minimum distribution requirements have been met, and which providers have received exchanges, or rollovers into the 403(b) accounts, and so on.

18

457(b) Compliance Checklist

The checklist will help employers that are planning to adopt or have already adopted 457(b) plans. It is important to note that responsibilities for the 457(b) plan may be greater for employers than responsibilities for 403(b) plans, since the employer owns the asset for the benefit of participants and beneficiaries—and because 457(b) plan assets are required to be held in trust (which can also be satisfied with qualified annuity contracts or custodial accounts), certain state trust laws may apply fiduciary responsibilities and employee education requirements.

EMPLOYER RESPONSIBILITIES

❏ Has your legal counsel checked state statutes that might apply to your 457(b) plan?

For example, do statutes require a specific number of different risk and reward investments, and are there specific requirements about educating employees?

❏ When you adopted your plan document, did you arrange with the provider of that document for plan amendment services?

It is important that plan documents be amended when necessary due to new legislation or regulation.

❏ Have you established the processes and procedures to authorize loans (if you permit loans in your plan) and review requests for unexpected emergency hardship withdrawals?

Some employers will delegate this responsibility to the product provider(s) or utilize the services of a TPA; others will appoint a committee of employees to review and authorize transactions.

❏ In selecting the providers of products or investments, have you conformed to any state statute dictating the types of core investment choices that must be provided?

❏ If you are planning to limit eligibility in the plan, have you communicated that limitation to the providers of products or investments?

Note that the universal availability requirement inherent in a 403(b) plan does not apply to 457(b) plans. Since there are no nondiscrimination requirements, employers can limit participation to specific groups of employees or can simply permit all employees to participate.

❏ Do the eligible employees understand that the employer is required to own the assets on behalf of employees and beneficiaries and that those assets are set aside (either in a trust or in a qualified annuity contract or custodial account) to protect those assets from the general creditors of the employer?

It is important that employees understand that the ownership of the assets is required by law, but that those assets can be utilized only for their benefit.

❏ Has education of employees been arranged (generally through the investment providers), not only to conform with any state statute requiring that education, but also to familiarize participants with the rules for 457(b) plans?

SYSTEMS AND ADMINISTRATION

❏ Does the salary reduction agreement (sometimes referred to as a participation agreement) remind employees that the agreement must generally be submitted before the first day of the month in which contributions will begin? Does it remind employees when calculations or confirmation of year of birth (if needed for those using the age 50+ catch-up contributions) are required as detailed below?

The investment or product providers, or the TPA, if any, should provide the agreements if you do not already have your own.

❑ Has the payroll system been set to reject any salary reduction agreement that would exceed the basic limit ($17,500 in 2013, as indexed) and
  • require a calculation if the final three-year catch-up is permitted in the plan, or
  • require that any employee utilizing the age 50+ catch-up confirms year of birth (if not tracked by the employer), and
  • specify that no participant is permitted to use both catch-ups in the same year?

19

Forms and ASBO Resources

This chapter includes information on the most pertinent resources available to employers who have completed the necessary activities to adopt and operate under the rules of written plans, but who have decided to make changes after the initial effective date of the final regulations.

Included is a brief description of those resources available in the 403(b) Retirement Plan Web Resource Center (at www.asbointl .org). The materials were, unless otherwise indicated, developed by the members of the ASBO Retirement Plan Council. The sample investment provider agreement is included in this chapter in its entirety, while the salary reduction agreement from the Resource Center has been slightly amended to reflect the employee's agreement to conform with compliance processes necessary to meet the requirements of the final regulations and, further, to reflect the limits for the 2013 tax year.

Note that the information and the available forms are provided as samples only, which may be amended by users with the aid of their legal counsel.

In all cases, readers are advised to consult with tax or legal professionals.

The following materials are available on the 403(b) Resources link (click on Publications and Resources at the top, then on 403(b) Resources; most of the listed items are in 403(b) Archives).

TPA Checklist: Questions to Guide Selection of a Third-Party Administrator

Demand has been high for this list of questions to assist school business officials in selecting a TPA once their districts have decided hiring a TPA is the most effective option.

403(b) Services and Service Provider Options: Reference Guide and Responsibility Matrix

Mark this two-part resource as square one in your decision-making process. The reference guide describes the different types of services and providers available to help you and your district comply with the new 403(b) regulations. The responsibility matrix is a straightforward chart to help you choose the services and providers that fit your district's needs.

Sample Questions to Guide Selection of Potential 403(b) Service Providers

How will you choose the best providers for your district? Do you know which questions to ask to help separate the wheat from the chaff? Take the mystery out of your selection with this list of sample questions to ask potential service providers.

Investment Provider Service Agreement (Copy Included Below)

Recognize the essential components of a contract specifying the duties and responsibilities of the school and the 403(b) service provider by utilizing this sample co-created by ASBO International's 403(b) Retirement Plan Council and Pennsylvania ASBO's IRS 403(b) Regulation Task Force.

403(b) Plan Document for Public Education Organizations

Pull it all together with inspiration from this model common plan document and adoption agreement, co-created by ASBO International's 403(b) Retirement Plan Council and Pennsylvania ASBO's IRS 403(b) Regulation Task Force.

Salary Reduction Agreement for 403(b) Programs with Worksheets (Copy Included Below)

Refer to this sample salary reduction agreement and accompanying worksheets, co-created by ASBO International's 403(b) Retirement Plan Council and Pennsylvania ASBO's IRS 403(b) Regulation Task Force when designing the necessary enrollment forms for your school's employees.

Orphan Accounts Responsibility Sorter

What is an orphan 403(b) account, anyway? Which are grand-fathered, which are not, and how does my school handle each type? Here are definitions, explanations, and concise charts to help you de-fine your school's information sharing responsibilities.

ERISA and Fiduciary Q&A

Do the final 403(b) regulations cause public education employers to become plan fiduciaries? This and other questions on the topic have been causing great concern among ASBO members. Here are answers to help alleviate the confusion.

INVESTMENT PROVIDER SERVICE AGREEMENT

(Sample for review by legal counsel. Intended to assist in requiring that investment providers agree to assume responsibilities to aid in compli-ance with the final 403(b) regulations.)

This Agreement, effective as of the date hereof, by and between _____ (the "Employer") and _____, ("Service Provider") sets forth the terms and conditions of the agree-ment between the Employer and Service Provider relating to services provided by Service Provider to the Employer in support of their 403(b) Retirement Plan (the "Plan"). The parties intend that Service Provider will provide certain services to the Employer, as needed, to support the Employer's Plan. In furtherance of this intention, the parties agree as follows:

Duties and Responsibilities of Service Provider

Service Provider shall:

1. Qualified 403(b) Accounts. Offer only investment products ("Accounts") that meet the requirements of Section 403(b) of the Internal Revenue Code of 1986, as amended from time to time, any regulations issued thereunder, and any other applicable state or federal law.
2. Communications. Assist in communicating the Plan to employees, including but not limited to presenting information about the Plan and available investment options at group meetings, responding to individual inquiries from employees, and providing the Employer with informational material describing the Plan.
3. Informational Materials. Prepare written notice of eligibility/ availability for distribution to employees, prepare and distribute materials that describe the Plan, including contribution limits, possible tax advantages and disadvantages, investment options, enrollment procedures, and other information necessary for participating in the Plan.
4. Forms. Prepare forms for Employer's consideration to facilitate enrollment and investment selection for Plan Accounts, including salary reduction agreements, Account applications, and beneficiary designation forms provided by Service Provider.
5. Individual Meetings. Provide individual meetings with employees, upon request, to explain the Plan, respond to questions or concerns about the Plan, discuss the impact of Plan participation on the employee, and assist with the completion of necessary forms and related documentation.
6. Online Participant Access. Provide employees online access to their Plan Accounts twenty-four hours a day, seven days a week, unless there is a routine update or an unanticipated event beyond the control of Service Provider.

7. Participant Statements. Send statements to participant's address of record no later than fifteen business days after the end of each calendar quarter. Participant may also obtain statements via the secure Service Provider website.

8. Employer Plan Reports. Prepare Plan reports based on participant records processed through Service Provider upon Employer's request, including information on the number of participants in each investment option, the total amount of assets and the beginning Plan balance, previously unreported contributions, and ending balance.

9. Disburse Contributions to Account Investments. Allocate all amounts received in good order from the Employer to Accounts selected by participants. Such allocation received in good order by Service Provider shall occur within one (1) business day of receipt from the Employer or the Employer's designee unless circumstances beyond the control of Service Provider justify a later transmittal. In no event shall allocations received in good order by Service Provider occur later than seventy-two hours of Service Provider's receipt of proceeds from Employer.

10. Plan Exchanges. Provide that when receiving assets in an exchange or transfer under the Plan, distribution restrictions are not less stringent than those imposed under the transferor contract and that the accumulated benefit (as defined in applicable income tax regulations governing 403(b) plans) under the receiving contract immediately after the exchange or transfer is at least equal to the accumulated benefit under the transferor contract immediately prior to the exchange or transfer.

11. Confidentiality. Service Provider agrees to maintain the confidentiality and/or privacy of all information about participants and employees provided by Employer and to provide Employer with documentation of Service Provider's relevant privacy policies. All information relating to providing services hereunder shall only be communicated to Service Provider representatives, Employer, or its designated representative.

12. Solicitation. Service Provider and its representatives shall comply with all pertinent written directives regarding the solicitation of employees of Employer.
13. 403(b) Provisions. Service Provider agrees to do the following:
    a. Advise employees of the annual deferral limits under Section 402(g) of the Code and, if the Plan accepts Employer contributions, of the annual limitations applicable under Section 415(c) of the Code and to provide calculations to determine eligible contribution limits upon request of any employee. Any such calculations will be based upon applicable federal and state rules and regulations. Service Provider shall certify the accuracy of any such calculations, subject to the accuracy of information provided by the employee.
    b. If permitted under the Plan, properly calculate the Maximum Allowable Contribution for employees who are utilizing the "catch-up" provisions of 402(g)(7) and/or 414(v) in accordance with the information provided to Service Provider by Employer and the employee.
    c. If permitted under the Plan, properly administer loans in accordance with applicable federal and state rules and regulations.
    d. Provide tax reporting and required notices to participants requesting distributions.
    e. Permit and process corrective distributions of excess deferral contributions and properly track and report and/or distribute excess 415(c) contributions in accordance with applicable IRS regulations where such excess deferrals or excess contributions have been identified by Service Provider or by Employer or Employer's designated representative.
    f. Withhold and report any federal and state taxes on any distributions made directly to any employee and/or his/her beneficiaries as appropriate.
    g. Provide notification to participants who are age 70½ that they may be required to take Required Minimum Distributions and calculate and distribute such amounts as may be required under the Plan and the Code.
    h. If permitted under the Plan, administer hardship distributions including (if applicable) notifying Employer of the hardship distribution with instructions for Employer to suspend all

elective deferrals by participant to all plans sponsored by Employer for six months.

i. Administer distributions and enforce distribution restrictions under Code Section 403(b).

j. Administer transfers and exchanges to the extent permitted under the Plan subject to Employer designation of authorized providers and products.

k. Provide information to Employer relating to 403(b) accounts held by Service Provider for participants in the event of an income tax audit subject to written authorization by Employer and/or participant (as applicable). For example:

   i. Annual listing of total contributions, by investment provider, for each year under audit

   ii. Annual listing of all participant distributions for each year under audit

   iii. Annual listing of outstanding participant loans for each year under audit

   iv. Annual listing of any participant-defaulted loans for each year under audit

   v. Annual listing of exchanges and transfers processed for each year under audit

   vi. Copies of IRS tax reporting information (Forms 1099-R) for all distributions and defaulted loans for each year under audit

Such information shall be provided electronically, in hard copy, or in a manner otherwise mutually agreed upon by Employer and Service Provider.

Duties and Responsibilities of Employer

Employer shall:

1. Determine Eligible Employees. Determine which employees of Employer are eligible to participate in the Plan and certify that the 403(b) program will be made available to all eligible employees as required under the terms of Code section 403(b)(12)(A)(ii).

2. Primary Contact Person. Appoint a primary contact person for purposes of implementing, administering, and coordinating any issues that may arise with respect to the Plan.

3. Transmit Contributions. Transmit all contributions to Service Provider in a time and manner acceptable to both parties and consistent with applicable income tax regulations.

4. Identify Investment Providers. Make available to all employees and Service Provider a current list of authorized investment providers and investment products (annuity contracts, custodial accounts, grandfathered life insurance contracts) available under the Plan.

5. Provide Information. Agree to furnish Service Provider, as soon as practicable, any and all information which Service Provider may require in order to fulfill its duties under this Agreement, including but not limited to information on employment status, any exchanges and transfers authorized by Employer or its representative, and information on any participant hardship withdrawals from other Accounts under the Plan.

6. Eligible Employer. Certify that it qualifies under Section 403(b) of the Internal Revenue Code of 1986, as amended, as an organization eligible to offer this 403(b) plan to its employees and accept all liability for this determination. Employer agrees to notify Service Provider if it becomes an ineligible organization.

7. Plan Document. Certify that it now maintains or will maintain a written plan in accordance with applicable IRS regulations and that, among other provisions, the Plan provides or will provide for exchanges between authorized product providers or investment options.

8. Plan Exchanges. Agree that Service Provider may accept an exchange of assets from another 403(b) account under the Plan.

9. Third-Party Administrator. Agree to notify Service Provider if Employer has allocated certain specified administrative responsibilities to a third party and, by so notifying Service Provider, authorize Service Provider to share necessary Plan information with the third-party administrator in a manner which is consistent with applicable privacy requirements under this Agreement and under applicable law.

10. Employer Contributions. If Employer makes nonelective contributions into the Plan, provide a listing of participants that are
receiving such contributions and the amounts allocated to each
participant with each remittance.

Both parties agree that the following terms and conditions are included as part of this Agreement:

1. Information Sharing. Each party agrees to provide information necessary to comply with the regulations under Section 403(b) of the
Code and the Plan, including information concerning the participant's employment status and information that takes into account
other Code section 403(b) contracts/custodial accounts and any
other information deemed necessary to ensure compliance including but not limited to information required for distributions from
the Plan, Plan loans, rollovers into the Plan, Plan-to-Plan transfers,
and Plan exchanges. Such information shall be provided in a form
and manner, and within time periods, as shall be agreed from time
to time between Employer and Service Provider.
2. Indemnification. Each party agrees, to the extent permitted by
applicable law, to indemnify and hold harmless the other party,
including any individual member of the governing boards, and
their employees, from every claim, demand, or suit which may
arise out of, be connected with, or be made by reason of the other
party's failure to meet the requirements of this Agreement. Notwithstanding the preceding sentence, this indemnification shall
not cover any claim, demand, or suit based on the willful miscon-
duct or fraud of either party or its employees. Either party shall,
at its own expense and risk, defend, or at its option settle, any
court proceeding that may be brought against it, members of the
governing board, and employees on any claim, demand, or suits
covered by this indemnification, and shall satisfy any judgment
that may be rendered against any of them with respect to any
such claim or demand, provided that such party notifies the other
party, in writing, within twenty (20) business days of receipt of
such claim or demand. Each party's liability hereunder shall be
limited to actual damages, including, where applicable, income

tax penalties (but not the taxes themselves) and out-of-pocket legal fees and expenses only.

3. Exclusive Services. Except as otherwise provided in this paragraph 3, this Agreement and the underlying contracts or accounts are the exclusive arrangement between the parties for services under the Plan and the terms of this Agreement do not extend beyond such program. Neither party shall have any other obligations or liabilities not specified herein unless both parties agree to such additional obligations or liabilities in writing.

4. Not Legal Advice. The parties agree that no service provided by the terms of this Agreement or under the Plan is to be construed as individual legal or tax advice to participants, nor to either party.

5. Term of the Agreement. This Agreement shall continue from year to year unless terminated by either party, in writing, by no less than sixty (60) days written notice.

6. Applicable Law. This Agreement shall be construed under the laws of the state where Employer's principal office resides, unless preempted by federal law. Any litigation with respect to the terms or conditions of the Agreement will be conducted under such state's jurisdiction and the parties agree that venue lies therein.

7. Severability. Each party agrees that it will perform its obligations hereunder in accordance with all applicable laws, rules, and regulations now or hereafter in effect. If any term or provision of this Agreement shall be found to be illegal or unenforceable then, notwithstanding, the remainder of this Agreement shall remain in full force and effect and such term or provision shall be deemed stricken.

By executing this Agreement, dated _____, each party acknowledges that it has read this Agreement and agrees to its terms.

Agreed to:

Employer: Service Provider:

Address: Address:

By: _____   By: _____

Authorized Representative   Authorized Representative

Title:_____   Title: _____

SALARY REDUCTION AGREEMENT

(Sample agreement for contributions made to a traditional and/or Roth 403(b) account. Includes limits for the 2013 tax year. Note that limits will change over time due to indexing. Users should check limits for each subsequent tax year. Note that worksheets for use in verifying the age 50+ catch-up contribution and the "15+ years of service" increased limit are available at the 403(b) Resources section of the ASBO website.)

Part 1. Employee Information

Name: _____ SS#: _____
Address: _____

Part 2. Agreement

The above-named Employee elects to become a participant of the Employer's 403(b) Plan and agrees to be bound by all the terms and conditions of the plan. By executing this agreement, Employee authorizes Employer to reduce his or her compensation and have that amount contributed as an elective deferral and/or as a salary reduction contribution to the Roth 403(b) option if permitted in the plan, on his or her behalf, into the annuity or custodial accounts as selected by Employee. It is intended that the requirements of all applicable state or federal income tax rules and regulations (Applicable Law) will be met. Employee understands and agrees to the following:

1. This Salary Reduction Agreement is legally binding and irrevocable with respect to amounts paid or available while this agreement is in effect;

2. This Salary Reduction Agreement may be terminated at any time for amounts not yet paid or available, and a termination request is permanent and remains in effect until a new Salary Reduction Agreement is submitted; and

3. This Salary Reduction Agreement may be changed with respect to amounts not yet paid or available in accordance with Employer's administrative procedures.

Employee is responsible for providing the necessary information at the time of initial enrollment and later if there are any changes in any information necessary or advisable for Employer to administer the plan. Employee is responsible for determining that the salary reduction amount does not exceed the limits set forth in applicable law. Furthermore, Employee agrees to indemnify and hold Employer harmless against any and all actions, claims, and demands whatsoever that may arise from the purchase of annuities or custodial accounts. Employee acknowledges that Employer has made no representation to Employee regarding the advisability, appropriateness, or tax consequences of the purchase of the annuity and/or custodial account described herein. Employee agrees Employer shall have no liability whatsoever for any and all losses suffered by Employee with regard to his/her selection of the annuity and/or custodial account. Nothing herein shall affect the terms of employment between Employer and Employee. This agreement supersedes all prior salary reduction agreements and shall automatically terminate if Employee's employment is terminated.

Employee is responsible for setting up and signing the legal documents to establish an annuity contract or custodial account. However, in certain group annuity contracts, Employer is required to establish the contract.

Employee is responsible for naming a death beneficiary under annuity contracts or custodial accounts. Employee acknowledges that this is normally done at the time the contract or account is established and reviewed periodically.

Employee is responsible for following all requirements imposed by the employer or designated Plan Administrator to confirm eligibility for loans, distributions, and any other transactions available under the terms of the employer's plan. Vendors are not permitted to make loans, transfers or exchanges, or hardship distributions without meeting the compliance requirements established by both the terms of the employer's plan and the compliance processes and procedures established to meet the requirements imposed by relevant Code and Regulation.

Part 3. Representation by Employee for Calendar Year—2009

A. Participation in other employer plans: (you must check only one)

_____ I do not and will not have any other elective deferrals, voluntary salary reduction contributions, or nonelective contributions with any other employer.

_____ I do participate in another employer's 403(b), 401(k), SIMPLE IRA/401(k), or Salary Reduction SEP. The following information pertains to all of my other employers for the current calendar year:

Includable Earnings $_____; Elective Deferrals and/or salary reduction contributions to a Roth 403(b) or Roth 401(k) plan $_____; Nonelective Contributions $_____.

B. I have not received a Hardship Distribution from a plan of this Employer within the last six months.

C. Maximum elective deferral or Roth 401(k)/403(b) salary reduction contribution: (you must check only one)

_____ My elective deferral/salary reduction contribution does not exceed the Basic Limit (the lesser of my includable compensation or $17,500).

_____ My elective deferral exceeds the Basic Limit; however, I am age 50 or older, and agree to conform to any requirements of my employer in order to utilize the "age 50+" catch-up contribution in the amount of $5,500. I am not eligible to utilize the increased limit under the "15-year rule."

_____ My elective deferral exceeds the Basic Limit; however, I am eligible to utilize both the additional catch-up provision for the "15-year rule" and the "age 50 catch-up provision" for this calendar year only. I understand that amounts in excess of the basic limit shall be allocated first to the "15-year rule" and next to the "age 50 catch-up provision."

Part 4. Voluntary Salary Reduction Information
(Check all that apply)

❏ Initiate new salary reduction   Please complete Part 5.
❏ Change salary reduction   This is notification to change the
                                               amount of my elective deferral to
                                               the new amount listed in Part 5.
❏ Change Funding Vehicle   This is notification to change my
   Provider   Funding Vehicle—complete Part 5.
❏ Discontinue salary   Please discontinue my elective
   reduction   deferral to the following Funding
                                              Vehicle:

                                     _____

                                     _____.

Implementation Date (next available pay on or after): _____
_____.

Part 5. Funding Vehicle and Amount of Pretax Elective Deferrals

Contribution per Pay
Period (Select One)*   *Funding Vehicles (Annuity Contracts or Custodial Accounts)*

1. ❏ _____ % or
   ❏ $ _____
2. ❏ _____ % or
   ❏ $ _____
3. ❏ _____ % or
   ❏ $ _____

Note: Any employee who works variable hours or who does not have a regular biweekly paycheck must select "% of pay."

Part 5a. Funding Vehicle and Amount of After-Tax Salary Reduction Contributions to the Roth 403(b)

Amount per Pay Period
(Select One)   *Funding Vehicles (Annuity Contracts or Custodial Accounts)*

1. ❏ _____ % or
   ❏ $ _____
2. ❏ _____ % or
   ❏ $ _____
3. ❏ _____ % or
   ❏ $ _____

Note that the combination of pretax deferrals and Roth 403(b) contributions cannot, in combination, exceed the limits in force for the specific tax year.

Part 6. Employee Signature

I certify that I have read this complete agreement and provided the information necessary for Employer to administer the Plan and that my salary reductions will not exceed the elective deferral or contribution limits as determined by Applicable Law. I understand my responsibilities as an Employee under this Program, and I request that Employer take the action specified in this agreement. I understand that I must conform to the terms of the Employer's written plan, and comply with the compliance procedures imposed by the Employer as required under both Code and Regulation.

Employee Signature: _____ Date: _____

Part 7. Employer Signature

Employer hereby agrees to this Salary Reduction Agreement.

Employer Signature: _____ Title: _____

Date: _____

About the Author

Ellie Lowder, a tax-exempt and governmental plan consultant (TGPC), can be contacted at elowder@gainbroadband.com. She has more than fifty years of experience in 403(b) plans and is the coauthor of *The Source: 403(b) and 457(b) Plans (NTSAA-ASPPA)*, as well as a number of retirement plan compliance manuals for public education employers. She also serves on the ASBO Retirement Plan Council, which has prepared substantial 403(b) resource materials (covered further in this book). She regularly communicates with the Internal Revenue Service to provide up-to-date information about IRS audit activities and practical compliance steps that school business officials can take to correctly operate their 403(b) arrangements.

www.ingramcontent.com/pod-product-compliance
Lightning Source LLC
Chambersburg PA
CBHW021604210326
41599CB00010B/587